The Good Heart

The Good Heart

101 Ways to Live a Positively Long, Happy Life

Austen Hayes, Ph.D.

First published by O-Books, 2012
O-Books is an imprint of John Hunt Publishing Ltd., Laurel House, Station Approach,
Alresford, Hants, SO24 9JH, UK
office1@jhpbooks.net
www.johnhuntpublishing.com

For distributor details and how to order please visit the 'Ordering' section on our website.

ISBN: 978 1 78099 525 0

A CIP catalogue record for this book is available from the British Library.

Design: David Kerby

Printed in the USA by Edwards Brothers Malloy

We operate a distinctive and ethical publishing philosophy in all
areas of our business, from our global network of authors to
production and worldwide distribution.

Introduction

At first, few people took me seriously. As a student research assistant at Florida's Miami Heart Institute in the early 1980s, I was aware of the curious glances if, when discussing patient care, I put the words "stress" and "heart disease" in the same sentence. At that time stress had nothing to do with it; heart disease was caused by smoking, diet, lack of exercise or genetics. (This, despite the work of cardiologists Meyer Friedman, M.D., and Ray Rosenman, M.D., who began writing about the "coronary-prone" personality theory—the idea that a cluster of personality characteristics has a mutual relationship with heart disease—as early as the mid-1950s.) A touchy-feely, guru-following hippie might talk about mind-body connections, but not the doctors. Not yet, anyway.

Still, as I measured a patient's blood pressure, I made mental associations between the numbers I observed and their personal demeanor. I saw a relationship between lower pressure for those who smiled and relaxed, and higher numbers for those who were irritable, tense and impatient. I believed that if I could convince the latter to take life less seriously, to keep things in perspective and be grateful for the health they had, I was sure they would improve. Maybe they could avoid or delay their need for pressure-lowering medications. If they could learn to manage their quick tempers and impatience, perhaps they would live longer.

During this same period, as an undergraduate psychology major, I discovered cognitive-behavioral therapy. It was love at first sight. This approach was a completely logical one and, in my opinion, most suitable for people with heart disease. According to the teachings of cognitive-behavioral therapy, what you think will influence the way you feel and behave. That meant there must be a link between the type of thinker you are, whether or not your perceptions will lead to anxiety, anger and depression, and, ultimately, if the arousal associated with those feelings would overtax the heart and vascular system. If patterns of thought influence emotion, and that emotion is negative, wouldn't a depressed or anxious person be less inclined to exercise or eat well or quit smoking? I began observing patients even more closely.

In the early 1990s I interned at the American Institute for Cognitive Therapy, in New York City. With the mentoring I received from the institute's founder, Robert Leahy, PhD., I strengthened my skills and resolve to bring hope to people with heart disease. Meanwhile, I met weekly with heart patients at Beth Israel medical Center, in New York. While there I was asked to present cognitive-therapy teachings to psychiatry residents. I opened my discussions with "It is believed that … " or "It is theorized … " I wasn't yet brave enough to say, "I believe …" for fear of getting the same quizzical glances I received at the Miami Heart Institute. Young medical students are skeptical. It was easier for me to just offer the facts. Talk of "stress" was still considered fluff, not accepted as an independent risk factor for heart disease. My colleagues would say, "Stress? That's nice, Dr. Hayes, but let's see what's really wrong with this patient: cholesterol, weight, family history …."

A decade later I had grown more confident. Without supervisors accusing me of "underpathologizing" patients as they had when I was in graduate school, I was able to incorporate positive psychology into my work. I had been taught to find weakness and fix it, but now I could also look for patients' strengths, the characteristics I believed would help them recover and regain self-confidence. I wanted to bring patients to the next step: introducing them to the protective and healing effects of positive emotions. It's one thing to introduce hard-driving, competitive and sometimes resistant heart patients to rational thinking, but how would they respond to the idea of thinking positively? I had learned enough about heart patients to know that they're not quick to trust. Heart patients are goal-directed. They want to hurry up and get the job done. That's what makes them achievers, what makes them great, what makes them want to do and be the best—no time wasted on "feelings."

Would these heart patients talk about kindness? Would they regard such discussions as a waste of time? Would they fear losing their edge?

I started presenting the emotional and physiological connection within discussions I knew these patients might be willing to participate, such as persistence, determination, resilience and industriousness—topics that opened the door for discussions of kindness, happiness and purpose. Patients learned to replace defensiveness with curiosity, envy with gratitude, and pessimism with hope. As each patient controlled blood pressure, exercised with greater enthusiasm and founds ways to make relationships more rewarding, the merits of rational thinking and a positive and optimistic outlook were clear.

One day, in my current position at the Mt. Sinai Medical Center, in New York City, it occurred to me that the patients entering the hospital's cardiac program were as uninformed about the relationship between thoughts, feelings, behaviors and heart disease as those I'd met 30 years earlier. Once clued in, Mt. Sinai's cardiac–support group participants gained physical and emotional confidence. Patients returned to weekly groups with stories of triumph over stress and improved mood. This model worked so well, how could it be that so few were aware of it? And how could I reach the 80 million in the U.S. alone, who have some form of cardiovascular disease? How could I get the attention of the 78 million baby boomers who would benefit from this approach as a way to prevent having a heart attack in the first place? Only about a third of those with diagnosed heart disease are referred to a cardiac rehabilitation program. Of that third, a small number have access to psychological services. Following hospitalization many return home feeling alone, frightened and confused.

In an attempt to rectify this learning gap my colleague, Patty Brownstein, R.N., then the administrator of the Mt. Sinai Cardiac Health Program, and I launched a Web site presenting the emotion-heart connection. We hoped to teach readers how to manage stress and anger, return to feelings of hope, and modify the aspects of their personalities that would maintain cardiac risk. We encouraged our online audience to continue with heart-healthy regimens long after the motivating effects of fear had worn away. Knowing that compliance has a lot to do with survival, we did all we could to stimulate a collaborative effort between patients, cardiologists and primary care physicians.

The project was more demanding and time consuming than we expected and we had to abandon it after three good years. The most popular feature of our Web site was our weekly tips that were sent to anyone interested in prevention or recovery, families of cardiac patients, and cardiac caregivers across the U.S., Canada, parts of Europe and Asia. We received incredible feedback from people who found our tips to be inspiring, reminding them to focus on what matters. Each tip combined my three decades spent with cardiac and non-cardiac patients, interwoven with the results of sound psychophysiological research.

How to get the word out? This book, a collection of those tips ... *The Good Heart*.

The Tips

1

Optimistic men and women with heart disease are less likely to experience a recurrence of any cardiac event such as a heart attack or angioplasty (Helgeson & Fritz, 1999). So how do you maintain an optimistic outlook when it seems everyone around you—the newscaster, your officemate, the person waiting in line beside you at the coffee shop—enthusiastically talks about how bad life can be? They might say, "The economy's a mess" or "People can't be trusted" or "Nobody cares about anything anymore" or "What's happened to the world" and on and on.

One way to hang on to your optimism is to think for yourself. Hold your own counsel. Practice balanced thinking. Look at all sides to a story before you choose the path of negativity. Can you see a situation differently? Can you find the good in what people complain about?

Also, observe. Pay attention to the person who smiles at you. Show appreciation to the clerk in the store who goes out of her way to find the item you're looking for. Tell the man in the bakery how grateful you are when he offers you the freshest, right-out-of-the-oven bread. Then, before you go to sleep at night, review the behaviors you noticed in others that made your day easier and more pleasant. If you take the time to express gratitude—which encourages others—and acknowledge even the smallest good deed, you'll be rewarded with an improved outlook on life.

The next time someone approaches you with negative news, remember that you're the master of your own opinions, you're in charge of your mind, your mood and your optimism.

2

The angrier you are, the greater the likelihood you'll develop heart disease. If you've already been diagnosed with cardiac illness, your anger may contribute to a first or second cardiac event. If you're young and you're angry, you may develop heart disease earlier in life than the average person your age. A recently published Harvard University study associated hostility with "poorer lung function and rapid rates of decline among older men."

Know yourself. What are the triggers that most frequently lead to feelings of anger? Try to avoid waiting until you're facing the things that most often lead to anger. Think ahead. Practice and rehearse before you reach your melting point. How will you respond to what bothers you most? For example, say to yourself, *I expect that when I get stuck in traffic I'll feel agitated and annoyed. But today I plan to handle this differently. Whether or not another driver does something that I don't like, I don't have to react. It's foolish of me to expect that every driver on the road will navigate the same way—my way. There are many different models of cars and many different types of drivers. Let me be the best driver I can be. My heart is too important.*

3

The way we think not only influences actions and feelings, it can change the biology of the brain. That's according to Norman Doidge's *The Brain That Changes Itself*, which supports what cognitive-behavioral practitioners so strongly believe. In the book Doidge notes changes in brain electric activity as individuals learned a series of notes on a piano. Other "learners"—sitting in front of, but not playing the piano—showed the same changes in brain activity. Thinking creates change. Often, the key to change is a willingness to try something new accompanied by an assumption that it will lead to success. If in the past you never saw yourself as active but now you're attending a cardiac-rehabilitation program and happily exercising on the treadmill three times a week, think about the possibilities for your mind! Change your self-view of a couch potato to a person who is energetic. Instead of thinking of yourself as stressed and intense, see yourself as calm and easy-going. As you change the way you view yourself, the actions that complement your new view will be carried out more regularly.

Your brain is listening, what are you saying?

4

Patients with "stable" coronary artery disease who were either depressed or anxious experienced a doubling of risk for a major cardiac event. Anxiety-prone individuals describe feeling apprehensive with their first morning breath. Fatigue, irritability, tension and constant thoughts about how to stop worrying overwhelm their body and mind. Conditioned by this chronic uncertainty, a cardiac–support group participant was heard saying, "When I wake up I ask myself, What is it I'm supposed to be worried about today?"

As with all negative emotional states, good health habits weaken as distress intensifies. Relief is more easily accomplished with a cookie than with a carrot stick. Anxious people often calm themselves with fats and carbohydrates, alcohol and cigarettes. Bad habits like these promote the development of atherosclerosis, but so will the arousal prompted by cascading stress hormones released as tension and fear worsen. The need to flee is evident in the constant state of vigilance and distraction felt by the anxious individual. There's a short-circuiting of concentration, attention, memory and an essential element of health—the ability to get a good night's sleep. Activities that quiet a restless mind and relax a tense body lose their appeal; it's almost impossible to bury oneself in a book when obsessing takes over; the pounding of your own heart can drown out music you love. So what can you do?

- When worry appears, acknowledge it. Tell yourself, *Here it is again*. Then let it be. Attempting to stop worry may increase i t s potency. Redirect your attention.
- Begin your day by writing about everything that's on your mind. Free-associate. Getting your thoughts onto paper may help to significantly reduce uncomfortable feelings. Don't b e concerned about how or what your write just write.
- Schedule "worry time." Today at 6:00 p.m. for 30 minutes, worry as much as you can. This paradoxical intervention can work wonders.
- Read *The Worry Cure: Seven Steps to Stop Worry from Stopping You* by Robert Leahy, Ph.D. This is an excellent guide, packed with distress-relieving techniques that'll help you better understand your particular type of anxiety.

5

Are you able to say "no?" If you spend your life trying to please everyone, you might wind up extending yourself beyond what is good for your heart. When the needs of others are more important than your own, tension, exhaustion and resentment are likely to follow. This physical and emotional combination is accompanied by cascading stress hormones that may contribute to long-term wear-and-tear on your cardiovascular system.

Have you earned the right to say "no" at least some of the time? When someone you know asks you to do something you would rather not do, pay close attention to your personal limitations of time and stamina. Experiment with a new response—a politely delivered "no."

6

Calvin Coolidge was quoted as saying, "Nothing in the world can take the place of persistence."

With a chronic cardiac condition, persistence means taking the medicine your physician has prescribed and not using feeling better or not feeling any different as an excuse to abandon your regimen. It means returning to your plan for good eating habits, even if yesterday you faltered and ate things that were not so heart-healthy. It means getting out to walk in spite of an inner voice saying, *I just don't feel like it.* It means maintaining your gym schedule even if you're thinking *I'll never get better. I'm too old, too ill, too tired.* It means staying steady and trying one more time when you think things will never improve.

If there's something you're struggling with today, some part of you that feels like giving up, go one more day, give it one more try and give it your best. At the end of the day ask yourself if persistence made a difference.

In his book *Keep Going* Joseph Marshall quotes a wise grandfather speaking to his grandson: "We only need to be strong enough to stand. Whether we stand shaking in fear or shaking our fist, as long as we stand, we are strong enough."

7

A recently published study of marital discord and its relationship to health suggests that bottling up feelings during an argument may have a very different effect on women than it does on men. The numbers of men and women who kept their feelings to themselves were similar (32% men; 23% women), but the women were four times more likely to die during the 10-year study period when compared with women who revealed their feelings to their spouse.

An article *in The New York Times* (October 2007) describing this study suggested that for the men, "silence" may be "a calculated but harmless decision to keep the peace.... But when women stay quiet, it takes a surprising physical toll."

Although husbands and wives may have appeared to respond similarly using silence, if we knew the perceptions each had regarding what it means to argue—no matter what the arguments were about—we might more fully understand the reasons for these differences. If, during the course of an argument, a husband is thinking, *There's no real point in responding*, he would appear to be bottling up his feelings. In fact, he may be buffering the effects of the stressful experience by keeping things in perspective. *There's no point in responding* might reflect the assumption that keeping the peace is better than winning the argument.

Maintaining perspective helps us to cope successfully, and effective coping supports good health. A woman's silence-producing thoughts may reflect assumptions such as, *If I say how I feel, he'll accuse me of being too emotional* or *If I tell him ... he'll get angry.* He may be coping, but she's avoiding. He may feel calm and detached, but she may feel resentful, and resentment and avoidance lead to tension, which can trigger a rise in blood pressure and constriction of blood vessels.

A husband and wife who keep their feelings to themselves as they argue might look the same, but their bodies are responding differently. If we were to ask them separately what it means to argue and why arguing is so difficult, we might understand more about why one spouse is far less likely to grow ill from the effects of the same experience. If we were to ask, "What do you think will happen if you tell your husband/your wife what you're feeling?" different answers, reflecting different perceptions, may reveal much.

Saying what you feel shouldn't get you in trouble and it may be another way to protect your health. Express yourself. One way to increase your chances of getting a positive response may be to follow an old, tried and true communication rule of thumb: What matters isn't what you say as much as the way in which you say it.

8

If you're accustomed to being in charge and completely independent, a diagnosis of heart disease can do a lot to undermine personal confidence. You know you've experienced a life-changing event and you wonder if things will ever be the same.

For baby boomers, 78 million strong, poor health is at the top of the list of things to fear. Aside from financial instability there is an almost universal fear of being dependent on others for our care.

As it turns out, illness does not always break us down—shifting health can mean shifting priorities. When what matters most begins to change, such as time with family rather than time spent getting richer, your lifestyle practices may improve, your health gets better and the best of who you are will be revealed. Believe it or not, illness, physical or psychological—heart disease usually incorporates both—may build character.Peterson, Park and Seligman (2006) observed a strengthening of positive traits following illness. Those experiencing physical challenges gained in measures of bravery, kindness and humor. Heightened appreciation of beauty and love of learning were found in people experiencing psychological problems.

When you've had a heart attack or in the weeks following coronary artery bypass surgery, bravery or beauty may be the last things on your mind. You might view yourself as weak, unsure, vulnerable or confused. Be patient. With your thoughts and with time you have an opportunity to make things better. How have you benefited from your illness? Do you view life differently now? How? If you consider heart disease a limitation, that's what you can expect. If you see it as a second chance, an opportunity to do things differently and take charge of your health, that's the way it will be.

9

Women are more physiologically and psychologically sensitive than men are to stress in the workplace. This includes the workload and the amount of control a woman feels she has in the work environment. Both of these may lead to burnout—a stressful condition for a woman's heart.

Try this: On the way to work, mentally rehearse how you're going to perceive the difficulties of the day. Is there a way to respond that will be effective, keeping you calm and helping your heart?

10

Life is unfair. You feel unappreciated. You give more than you get. Others seem critical and rejecting. You're quick to argue or disagree with people. Your mood makes it difficult for you to stop smoking. To soothe bad feelings you eat more sweets, drink more alcohol and eat more fat. You drive impulsively, sometimes aggressively. You've had a few bouts of road rage.

If you made a list of all the things you believe cause you to feel angry, what would be on the list? People who are inconsiderate? People who drive too slow or fast? People who make mistakes? People who take advantage of others? People who talk on their cell phones in public places? Big banks? The auto industry?

Add to your list *The way I feel about myself.* Anger and self-esteem have a strong inverse relationship—the less you have of one, the more of the other. If not feeling good about your self isn't enough to contend with, remember that chronic anger can negatively impact your health. With negative emotion comes more risk to the integrity of your cardiovascular system in the form of constriction, raised pressure, platelets that clump and damaging turbulence within artery walls. When it comes to your health, it's your heart that must be taken seriously, rather than all those people who don't do things the right way.

If the next time a driver cuts in front of you and you feel as if you're about to blow up, ask yourself, *What does this mean to me?* If the answer is something like, *That driver thinks he can take advantage of me* or *Just because my car isn't as expensive as hers, she thinks I'm a nobody* or *They're not getting away with this, they can't do this to me— I'm too important* ... it isn't about bad drivers as much as it is about your self-worth.

No matter what another person has done, is their lack of good behavior a measure of your worth? If you think it is, you're bound to feel angry. No one can give or take away your value. It just doesn't work that way.

11

Phobias have recently been added to the many emotional states that can put your heart at risk. As a part of the ongoing Nurses Study (Albert, 2005), women with phobias were found to have a 31% increased risk of developing coronary artery disease and a 59% greater risk of death due to heart attack.

This isn't surprising. The fear associated with a phobic response can trigger a series of physiological reactions, including increased blood pressure and cardiac output, turbulence throughout the cardiovascular system and constriction of vessels, compromising blood flow. Over time this may lead to deterioration of the cardiovascular system and, in a moment of intense fear, something far more serious.

Phobias come in many forms: fear of heights (falling); the outdoors (loss of control); flying (crashing); elevators or tunnels (being trapped); insects or snakes (being bitten). Some people fear taking medication for high blood pressure, afraid the medicine will cause a sudden rise in pressure or cause a heart attack. Some people fear taking an antidepressant, afraid of losing control once medicine is in the body, particularly in the brain. These fears may not make much sense, but they're real to the person who has them.

If fear limits your life—if you avoid elevators despite living in a city packed with high-rises, or you avoid driving through tunnels though bypassing the one on your commute adds hours to your drive—seek treatment. A technique known as "exposure" helps an anxious patient to differentiate between being uncomfortable and being in danger.

Choosing to meet something you fear head on is easier than having it intrude on your life. Your heart is listening to your thoughts. Are you telling your heart to be fearful?

12

A recent study determined that severely anxious men without any indication of heart disease at the start of a 12-year investigation had more heart attacks than their less anxious peers.

Until recently, most emotion-driven associations to heart disease have focused on Type-A personality, depression and hostility with little said about anxiety. All negative emotional states, especially those considered chronic or severe, will trigger potentially damaging physiological reactions, such as increased blood pressure, vessel constriction and increased potential for clotting. The overall discomfort felt by a man or woman suffering with obsessive thinking, irrational compulsions, social introversion, phobias or somatic complaints, such as tension, leaves little doubt that chronic arousal can do much to chip away at good health. Does that mean the anxiety-prone individual will seek treatment that we now know might reduce the possibility of having a heart attack?

Anxious people are self-conscious and focus inward. They often think of themselves as weak, abnormal or weird. They view their symptoms as strange and too embarrassing to reveal. So instead of getting help, they may become more avoidant. An obsessive individual can hide intrusive thoughts. A phobic person will avoid a feared object or situation. Socially introverted people learn to turn down invitations. Some anxious people feel relieved after concluding that their inner tension is hard for others to detect. But the longer symptoms and fears are successfully hidden, the longer it takes before help is secured, which means the longer the problem lasts and the worse it may become.

Prevention depends on your willingness to talk with caregivers about cholesterol, exercise, smoking, diabetes or unusual or worrisome physical symptoms. It's also critical to discuss doubts and fears. There's nothing strange about anxiety. The health of your heart is far more important than what others think of you.

13

As a Child, Albert Einstein found that learning to play the violin became easier once he had "fallen in love with Mozart sonatas." Later, he said, "I believe, on the whole, that love is a better teacher than sense of duty."

Einstein's youthful struggles had nothing to do with ability, but, rather, motivation. When we don't like what we're doing, sense of duty is the experience and avoidance the response. Whatever you choose as your route to health and fitness—running on a treadmill, meditation, tennis, playing with your dog or rock climbing—loving what you do makes it so much easier.

According to positive psychologist Mihaly Csikszentmihalyi, "flow," or "complete absorption in what one does," happens when we choose activities related to our interests rather than "imposed demands." If your goal is to strengthen your heart and revive your cardiovascular system, being in "flow" might mean taking a daily two-mile walk through a beautiful countryside or through lively city streets—alive with every step, grateful for all you see, enjoying the activity so much that the goal is almost forgotten. For some, it might mean getting lost in the sound of your feet rhythmically striking a treadmill.

Try as many different activities as necessary to find what's right for you. When you find yourself intensely focused on what you're doing and time seems to slip by, it's likely you're in "flow." The best part: the encouragement you feel to persist at what you're doing, to return to the health-promoting activity tomorrow and the day after that, because you want to.

14

Much of the distress of life is related to our perception of the unfairness of things. If we spend too much time asking *What about me? Why not me? Where's mine? How could he do this to me?* it's unlikely that we're recognizing the needs of others and responding to the feelings of those we deal with each day. Some people might think we lack warmth or the ability to sympathize. They may be right. Survival and the ability to care about others are absolutely connected. When a limited supply of something good to eat is presented to a group of primates, a primate leader will see to it that each group member gets a portion of what is available. Primates have the ability to recognize the needs of other primates and do something about it to ensure group survival.

Rather than approach life with a *What about me?* attitude, consider practicing a more giving, generous *What about you?* attitude. If your first thought is that those around you are ready to take advantage of you or that they see you as weak, test your assumption: list the times when people have shown consideration for your needs or gone out of their way to be helpful or generous. If you're really brave you might even ask them how they see you. If you're frequently *thinking I, me, mine,* try practicing something different: imagine how others feel. Imagine how you would feel if you were facing the same trials as those around you. Consider how the things you say to a store clerk, a waiter, a neighbor or a loved one affects them the rest of the day. If a self-absorbed, self-protecting life is driven by a fear of losing out or being taken advantage of, perhaps true advantage comes when we practice consideration of others.

15

When someone tells us something outrageous we roar with laughter, shouting, "You're killing me!" or "Stop! You're going to give me a heart attack!" or as Fred Sanford of the 1970s sitcom "Sanford and Son" would say as he looked to the heavens clutching his chest, "Elizabeth, this is the big one!" We joke about it, but is it really possible to hear news so devastating or experience an event so frightening that we could drop dead of a heart attack?

At the moment of an intense reaction, for example, learning of the death of a loved one, stress hormones can overwhelm the cardiovascular system triggering a response known as "broken-heart syndrome." It's a response often, but not exclusively, seen in post-menopausal women.

Symptoms mimic those of a heart attack: shortness of breath, chest pain, low blood pressure and, possibly, heart failure. It's not a heart attack and, in most cases, there's no indication of cardiac disease. According to scientists at Johns Hopkins University, the heart has been stunned, not damaged. A distinct calling card of broken-heart syndrome is a change in the shape of the heart. Symptoms, including change in shape, are temporary with full recovery realized in a matter of days.

The unexpected is just that—out of the blue, sometimes amazing, sometimes heart-breaking. No life escapes the unanticipated but that doesn't mean everyone will experience a broken heart. It means that it's essential to value a fit body, sound thinking, stable emotions and a steady response.

16

Our country has a color-coded warning system in the event of an enemy attack. Billboards and Web sites remind us of the importance of being prepared. There are hurricanes, viruses and tainted foods. Fortunately, life-threatening experiences rarely happen. In fact, most threats we experience are social rather than physical.

We worry more about status, wealth, attractiveness and possessions than we do about terrorists. The things that occupy our minds might be not getting a promotion, the friend who takes forever to return calls, the neighbor whose car is newer and nicer, the co-worker who looks better, the smarter colleague, the old friend earning more money....

If you compare yourself to others—what they have, how they live, where they go, the first-class treatment they receive—and you see yourself in these mental competitions as the loser, you'll have many opportunities to react with the same heart-pumping arousal felt when a speeding car misses you by an inch. Never underestimate the power of social threat when it comes to developing inflammation and artery-clogging plaque. First you get just a bruised ego, but over time it's a damaged body.

For the good of your heart, celebrate your neighbor's success. Think of all possible reasons your friend failed to call, other than it pointing to something lacking in you. The person who compares, fears she'll never have enough. The person who gives, knows she has more than she needs.

17

In the months following a cardiac event, patients often talk about slipping back into old habits. As fear and disbelief associated with a heart attack or emergency bypass surgery subside, so can the motivation for essential lifestyle adjustments. Permission-giving assumptions roam freely: *Bad things happen to other people, not me. Just one piece of cake or hamburger, just one cigarette. A week without exercising can't hurt.* So why is it so difficult to stay on course when independence, mobility and life itself depend on how we behave each day?

Human behavior is more easily understood when we think of it as "multi-determined." Action doesn't result from a single trigger, but rather a combination of variables, such as cues, intentions and mindfulness. But how does this relate to unhealthy habits?

Ellen Langer (2005) states, "The mindful individual is likely to choose to be positive and will experience both the advantages of positivity and the advantages of perceived control for well-being." There are cues all around us leading us astray if our intentions aren't firm or if we live without a plan or if we live mindlessly. A cue might be the sight of colorful frosted fatty foods in a bakery window, the lure of a cocktail after a tough day at the office, the smell of a burning cigarette as a smoker walks by on the sidewalk—cues that beckon when we're mindless. That's what slipping back is: automatically responding to cues—not thinking or being aware.

If you rehearse your actions and prohibit yourself from being cue-ruled, you'll succeed at self-regulation. Say to yourself, *When I shop today I'll bypass the cookies.* Envision yourself skipping the aisle altogether. Without this plan you automatically enter the zone of sugar and hydrogenated oils.

Or tell yourself, *I intend to walk a mile each morning this week.* Envision yourself strolling and enjoying it fully. Back up your intention by placing your walking clothes next to your bed so they're the first things you see when you wake up. Without this plan you'll find yourself in front of the television watching the morning news. If you become angry sitting in traffic jams, tell yourself, *Today my response to traffic will be slow deep breaths.* Strengthen your intention with a sticky-note on your dashboard that says, *Breathe!* Without this plan you'll respond with the usual rage when someone suddenly pulls out in front of you.

Practice mindfulness, choose intentions, develop new cues and say to yourself, *Today I will …*

18

Having high standards, a strong work ethic and dogged determination to reach every goal you've ever set for yourself may be admirable, but it may also lead to confusion and self-doubt if your life-plan is suddenly and dramatically derailed.

From the first day we go to school, planning is encouraged. Being a good planner is associated with reward. If you think ahead you'll be prepared, you won't be caught off guard. Indeed, most good outcomes depend on a plan, but an equally valuable trait is the ability to change course when you need to.

Heart disease isn't included in anyone's plan. No one prepares to have a heart attack. No one creates a "Plan B" just in case they develop heart failure. Perhaps you expected to work another 10 years, until age 70, but now must retire at 60. Prior to a diagnosis of heart disease you may have enjoyed complete independence. Now you have to depend on family and friends for help. You long for control.

Research shows that people over the age of 50 regained control when they were able to "de-emphasize the importance" of goals they felt were no longer achievable and devise new, "reachable" goals. It's all about perspective—finding the good, practicing appreciation for what is, making life itself more important than any plan.

19

Within the field of psychology, humility is not easily measured, but you know it when you see it. Humble people are unassuming and seem a little unsure—the opposite of the person who is always right and knows everything about everything.

Don't be fooled. What appears to be overly obliging or submissive behavior may conceal strength. It takes courage to say, "I don't know." Gentle open-mindedness is not weakness. It aligns with cooperation and generosity, characteristics known to support health and long life.

We recognize the truly confident man—he never tries to impress us with greatness. We easily identify the self-assured woman—she treats everyone as if they matter.

20

Having a positive view of age may actually slow the aging process and help you maintain good health. When subjects in a study (Lupien & Wan, 2005) were introduced to positive views of aging, cardiovascular stress was lessened. Negative comments about age are related to the development of health problems and shortened lifespan. Do you find yourself saying things like, "What do you expect at my age?" or "I'm not as young as I used to be" or "When you're as old as I am?" If so, you may be talking your body into a hastened state of decline.

If today you imagined yourself to be 10 or 15 years younger, how would you feel? Would you behave differently? Would you walk faster? Would you respond to life with greater enthusiasm? Would you bounce back more quickly from the things that bother you? Would you think differently about the future? Would you be interested in learning something new?

However you imagine yourself, and whatever words you use to describe yourself—old, exhausted, falling apart—will influence your heart, your memory, your confidence, your performance and your mood.

If a student assumes she's unlikely to do well on a test, because math isn't her best subject, her performance suffers. Likewise, if you tell your heart that it's unlikely to work well because it's too old and too tired, how will it perform? Thoughts are powerful. Thoughts "change brain structure" (Doidge, 2007). And, without a doubt, thoughts change the structure of your heart.

21

During a radio program about economic challenges, a woman called in to say she felt relieved after losing her job. "Not knowing if or when I would be let go was worse that being fired," she said. "Now I know where I stand."

These are uncertain times. People are losing homes, jobs, health care, retirements, savings and personal control.

If, on a single occasion, your heart beats wildly and your doctor doesn't know why, you may feel more frightened than if you'd experienced a quadruple coronary bypass procedure. The difference between a mysterious change in the rhythm of your heart and surgery is a lack of certainty about just what could be wrong with you. If, following a successful stent implantation, you're recovering well and then one day your breath feels more labored than usual during a workout, your optimism might be replaced with uncertainty.

How do you handle uncertainty? The answer to that question may reveal something about your nervous system and your mental health.

According to experts in a recent study, responding to uncertainty more intensely than you would to a negative but certain outcome may be indicative of psychological problems. A measure included in personality tests—"neuroticism"—refers to someone who tends to be anxious, depressed, obsessive—someone easily upset by the ups and downs of everyday living. Research participants with high neuroticism scores had elevated neural activity if feedback, related to completed tasks, indicated an uncertain performance. Participants with lower neuroticism scores showed no differences in the way they responded to "uncertain" or "negative" feedback.

If you feel that your uncertainty is less than tolerable, try the following:

- Pay attention to your predictions. Are you expecting only negative outcomes? Balance your thinking by making a list of the positive possibilities. If you have a lengthy roster of negative predictions, use problem solving. Write down the ways you would handle a negative outcome. What are your options? You may never need to use these options, but if you've listed them, that alone may be comforting.
- Develop a new assumption about uncertainty, a new rule to live by: *I don't like uncertainty, but I can handle it.* Or: *Not knowing for sure is uncomfortable, but it's manageable and usually temporary.* The more you practice the new rule, the more dependable it will be and the more confident you'll feel.
- Maintain a good perspective: *I'm unsure about this particular situation, but there's plenty in my life I can count on.*
- In *The Worry Cure, Seven Steps to Stop Worry from Stopping You,* author Dr. Robert Leahy suggests that as you begin to worry, "The first thing you can do is ask yourself, Is there some action I need to take now? If there is, then you can turn your worry into problem solving, rather than look for more problems or for the perfect answer."

22

Optimism is a good thing, but behavioral scientists also suggest that being optimistic may not be linked to everything positive, after all. For example, individuals found to have "optimistic bias" (Weinstein, 1989) are thought to "neglect the basics of health promotion and maintenance" due to an unshakable belief in their ability to avoid illness and trauma. Studies indicate that those with high levels of optimistic bias and an overall optimistic disposition are found to exercise less than others (Davidson & Prkachin, 1997). All of this refers to the bad-things-happen-to-other-people-not-me kind of thinking. There's a difference between being so optimistic that we assume we'll never break down, never get sick, never have anything bad happen to us versus understanding what good health is all about. It's about what we do to preserve it. Eighty percent of what leads to heart disease is related to lifestyle (smoking, hypertension, not exercising and failing to manage stress)—behavior choices that in the end are ours and ours alone to manage.

Positive psychologists encourage optimism, but do not confuse optimism with denial. Anyone can develop heart disease. Further, those who have already been diagnosed with heart disease or survived a cardiac event, such as a heart attack or bypass surgery can't afford to be so optimistic that they return to their old habits of too many hamburgers, cigarettes and chronic stress.

Make the best use of your positive outlook: Let it be the strength that gets you up and out for a walk on a less-than-perfect morning. Let it be the strength that allows you to keep things in perspective when the day seems to be falling apart. Let it be the strength that allows you to feel encouraged, enthusiastic and anticipating the best in spite of adversity. But don't let it fool you into thinking that you can do whatever you please and you'll still be fine. Let all that you do be a reflection of how much you value your health, your heart and the opportunity you've been given—to live.

23

There is growing acceptance in the medical community about the link between depression and heart disease. This isn't a surprise to anyone who's ever experienced a bout of depression. If you were to ask them where their sadness was felt, a hand held to the chest says it all.

Depression sends the body into a downward spiral with the same constriction of blood vessels, rise in blood pressure, increased levels of unhealthy fats in the bloodstream and turbulence within artery walls experienced by people who are hostile, anxious or fearful. Personal habits begin to deteriorate as the depressed individual grows more withdrawn and less active. Memory fails, concentration and attention are poor, and a rational inner dialogue needed to lift the depressed individual up and out of despair disappears.

It's time for action, not just thought. "There is support for a causal link between physical activity and reduced clinically defined depression" (Biddle et al., 2000). Is it possible to find a renewal of hope in a 10-minute walk? Absolutely.

If you've been diagnosed with heart disease while experiencing depression, the risk of a cardiac event, such as a heart attack, or need for life-saving procedure, such as angioplasty, is far more significant than with a diagnosis of heart disease alone. If you're sad most of the time, if you cry easily or you've lost interest in activities that you once enjoyed, rather than thinking about how awful you feel, take action: let your primary care physician and cardiologist know what's going on.

24

One way to avoid feeling helpless is to be productive, to accomplish something. You can't waste time or make mistakes. Order and control are critical. Letting things get out of order means chaos, and being out of control is scary. Relaxing when you should be accomplishing things is unacceptable.

Is this you? Is this how you think?

What are the things you don't have time for? Reading a novel? Taking a vacation? Getting to know someone? Being a good listener? Kicking back in a hammock? Spending time with your children? Sure, everyone is busy and time is scarce. We're all absorbed with making money, consuming what we buy, taking care of what we own, cleaning up after ourselves, then doing it all over again. Productive people are rewarded. They're admired, paid more and in demand.

The sense of control that comes with completing a task or project helps ward off feelings of anxiety. As actions are rewarded and reinforced, the drive to accomplish grows, but the hours in a day never do. Perhaps there's no end to your list of things to do, so there's no end to the obsessing and pressured feelings. But you keep trying. You do all you can to keep up. You squeeze in more and more and eliminate activities that don't produce something, such as interactions with those who might add to your sense of well-being and fulfillment.

It's no surprise that this type of stressful living isn't heart-healthy. It's not relationship-healthy or life-healthy. Chronic pressure— always feeling behind and rarely living in the present—may mean high arousal, chronic tension and neglected relationships.

Ask yourself: Are you in the here and now or is your mind on all the things that are piling up inside your mind and body? Break the cycle by trying the following:

- As you're doing a particular task remind yourself, *At this moment this is all I must do, all I need to concentrate on. There's nothing else. I'll think about the next task as I'm doing it—later, not now.*
- Conduct a behavioral experiment. For one day follow

your usual routine. The second day take time to relax for approximately one hour (you'll be surprised how challenging this is). Compare the two days to see how much has been accomplished. Is there a difference?

25

Autonomy is strength. Self-determination means freedom.

Must you regularly compare yourself with others? Is it helpful? You have little freedom when your life is guided by a persistent need for outside approval. What do you think? What is your opinion?

Proving yourself maintains and strengthens feelings of low self-worth. As human animals, low self-worth is often accompanied by a need to please others, to impress others, to outdo others. In a socially unstable environment, primates reposition themselves: they act to reestablish dominance when introduced to a new cage mate, and end up with coronary artery disease. Is proving that you're bigger, better, smarter, richer and faster worth more than your health? Your life?

26

When women join cardiac-support groups they tend to do better in a group that only includes one gender—theirs. Women in mixed groups speak up less and ask fewer questions.
See if you can find a woman's cardiac-support group in your area.

If there isn't one, ask the nurse in your doctor's office or the social worker in the hospital if there might be a professional who would consider—with your help—starting such a group. Group support, education and stress management may contribute in a significant way to a reduction in cardiac events for patients with coronary heart disease.

27

We explain a lot of what we do, even the relatively small decision we face each day, based on how we feel: "I didn't answer the phone—I wasn't in the mood." Or, "I was feeling too down to go to the gym." Unfortunately, when it comes to larger, life-changing decisions about things that dramatically affect our lifestyles, we still engage in emotional reasoning. Would you trust a decision processed through a filter of negativity and clouded thinking? What if you have to make an important decision that affects your life and because of depression, you lack the clarity to make a good one?

For eight years researchers followed late- to middle-aged individuals (from 53–58 at the start of the investigation) to determine the impact depression would have on their decisions about when to retire (Doshi, et al., 2008). Given the choice, depressed men and women were more likely to retire than their non-depressed peers. Women with only a few depressive symptoms, known as sub-clinical depression, were inclined to choose retirement over the workplace. What does this have to do with heart disease? When retirement is part of a positively anticipated plan, it can be a lively, creative time of life. Decided at a low point, motivated by a wish to escape, there may be no plan. And once retired, rather than anticipated relief, the depressed retiree may feel more distress. Isolated, without goals or interests, negative symptoms worsen. Depression often leads to personal neglect, allowing an increase of unhealthy habits, such as poor diet, lack of exercise, smoking and excessive alcohol consumption.

If you're struggling with a major decision and you feel depressed, the most valuable decision you can make is to find the help you need. Exercise, psychotherapy, medication—any combination depending on your psychological and biological makeup—can make an enormous difference in health and quality of life. Until you secure the guidance you need, exercising, even a small amount, is a great place to begin. Exercise has been found to lower the likelihood of relapse (relapse rate 9%) more than therapy or therapy and medication in combination (relapse rate 30%) (Blumenthal, et al., 1999).

Retirement isn't good or bad. But it should be the right choice for you. The heart flourishes when life is satisfying and offers reasons to get out of bed each morning. The office or the garden? Decide wisely with a clear mind and an open heart.

28

A woman called my office, inquiring about cardiac support groups. There was anxiety in her voice. "Since my heart surgery I've lost my confidence," she said. "I need help."

Through the years I've also heard: "I'm afraid to get up on a chair to replace a light bulb." "Can I stretch my arms that far?" "Is it safe to walk now?" "How far should I go?" "I'm afraid to get on the bus by myself." "Is it OK to fly, to travel? "I don't want to be too far from my doctor." "I'm afraid to go to sleep." Before their heart attacks or surgeries, these patients considered themselves able and independent.

Most of the questions patients have—the ones they feel anxious about—can be answered by physicians and nurses. But learning to trust your body is a personal matter. It takes time to rebuild confidence. The following are suggestions for doing just that:

- Join a cardiac–support group. Hearing the experiences of other heart patients can be inspiring.
- Ask your cardiologist or primary-care physician for a cardiac rehabilitation "prescription." Monitored exercise will make you feel more secure.
- Ask your doctor or nurse for exercise guidelines. Prepare a

written plan. For example, five to 10 minutes of daily walking, with small increases each week.
- Find a walking partner. Being with someone can distract you from negative thoughts.
- Carry a cell phone for added peace of mind.
- Think of sleep as healing rather than something to fear. Allow your heart to rest.
- Recovery isn't a race, it's the beginning of a lifetime of better health. You can do this with persistence, determination and the belief that with each step you take your confidence will return.

29

Abraham Lincoln said a man is about as happy as he makes up his mind to be. We may be as healthy as we expect to be. Optimists— those whose lives aren't any easier than yours but who expect good—make better use of health information. They take medicine as prescribed, choose heart-healthy foods and walk when they'd rather sit. They cope with discomfort and roll with life's ups and downs. They avoid self-pity, worry less and heal more quickly. Hope fosters the solid foundation for prevention of future illness.

If you expect: to feel more fit today than yesterday, you will; that your doctors care about you, they will; to feel invigorated when you exercise, you will; to be in a good mood as you start the day, you will; or that this will be a good day, it will.

Experiment. For an entire week look for all the not-so-good things that can happen—things that will go wrong and all the not-so-good ways you'll feel. The following week do the opposite. Begin each day with all the things you expect will go well and all the ways that you'll feel energetic, enthusiastic and open-minded.

30

Renowned psychologist Carl Rogers believed that people know what they need in order to "actualize" their full potential. Rogers thought we should never fear having faith in ourselves and our ability to know what really matters.

"Self"-determination is a key to fulfillment. If much of your life is "other"-determined with self-doubt driving a need for approval, you've found the key—to disappointment. Someone responds positively and you feel good about yourself. Someone responds negatively or not at all and suddenly you feel inadequate.

It's all about worth—yours. Follow your instincts. What do you believe is right for you? Strive for authenticity. Relying on others' approval means loss of freedom and chronic self-consciousness. *What do they think of me? What would they do? How do I look? They think I'm dumb. I don't measure up.*

There's little time left to reach your full potential when so much time is spent thinking about what others are thinking about you.

31

Optimists are accused of looking at life through rose-colored glasses. They're thought to miss the real picture, to fool themselves into seeing only the good side of life. Of course, everything has another side, no matter which side you happen to be on. Scientists have shown that optimists seem to be healthier than pessimists. If you ask 20 heart patients what it means to be diagnosed with hypertension, you may get 20 different responses ranging from "It's no big deal" to "This is the beginning of the end!"

Increasingly, members of the medical community talk about the way the body "listens" to thought. In other words, what we tell ourselves will be "heard" by the body and reflected in the way the respiratory, cardiac, digestive and immune systems respond and function. If a diagnosis of heart disease is filtered through negative expectations, the body is more likely to respond in ways that hinder rather than promote a best possible medical outcome. This is no time for pessimism. Dr. Herbert Benson, of Harvard University, suggests that when "the belief and expectations of the patient, the belief and expectations of the physician or health professional and the belief and expectations that come from the relationship of the two" are in agreement, "remarkable healing properties come about. If you believe yourself to be well, you can often be well."

Try to create an alternate, life-enhancing, life-giving belief. Don't be afraid to expect something good. A pessimistic golfer I know tells me he always says to himself, *Don't hit the ball into the lake.* With that, he hits the ball directly into the lake. Is it possible that his brain can't see the word "don't" and only envisions "into the lake?"

32

Following cardiac surgery or a heart attack, what you expect may influence recovery. Hope buffers the effects of stress and encourages action, such as taking medication, participating in a program of cardiac rehabilitation, making heart-healthy food choices or walking on a less-than-perfect day.

Hopeful people tend to make better use of health information. They cope with discomfort and adapt well to the responsibilities involved in the process of recovery. They're less inclined to feel self-pity, they worry less and heal more quickly. Hope is what you need when you strive for prevention of future illness.

Are you short on hope? Make a list of everything there is to feel hopeful about: family, your mind, an upcoming season, feeling strong again, the care you receive from your physician, the kindness of strangers, things you'd like to learn, the basic instinct we have to survive.

33

In a review of scientific studies on the subject of personality, mood and heart disease we're reminded of the critical need to attend to the style of our thinking. Thoughts influence emotions, emotions influence behavior, and both influence your heart. Cardiac behavioral scientist, Johan Denollet, reports that individuals at higher risk for developing cardiac disease "have an attention bias towards adverse stimuli" and "seem to scan the world for signs of impending trouble." A tendency to expect the worst may be the result of an inherited temperament or early learning: you were born with this tendency or perhaps you observed your parents refer to the downside of life more than the upside.

Whatever the cause, patterns of thought, or ways of looking at life, can be modified. Being open-minded, flexible and willing to see the other side can do much to improve mood. For example, a self-critical comment might be followed by something positive: *I never stick to anything. I didn't exercise all week and I ate really badly.... That may be true, but I did very well last month. I have to give myself credit for the efforts I've made!*

If your predictions are usually negative, think of positive possibilities as well: *Now that I've had a heart attack my life will be so limited. It's all downhill from now on....* That's not true. *Yes, I did have an attack but I'm feeling stronger each day. I'm grateful for the things I'm still able to enjoy!*

Search your mind for the positive alternative. It takes dedication and repetition to change a long-held pattern of negativity, but it's worth the effort. If you have heart disease or your goal is prevention, a better mood acts as a protective buffer between you and the stress of the day.

Dr. Martin Seligman suggests this simple, cost-free and effective mood-lifting exercise: At the end of the day, for three weeks, write down three things that went well with three reasons why, for each item on your list.

34

Novelist Eleanor H. Porter's 1913 *Pollyanna*, named for its resilient and relentlessly optimistic heroine, also known as the "Glad Girl," was the subject of a *Journal of Positive Psychology* article (October 2007) by Murray Levine. Among the many uplifting ideas offered by Pollyanna, writes Levine, "Most generally it doesn't take so long [to find something to be glad about]."

Your tendency toward pessimism or optimism—that's just who you are, you might say—reflects your disposition at birth combined with a lifetime of learning. In spite of a positive, or "glad," outlook, a diagnosis of heart disease may temporarily modify your mood downward and, surprisingly, if you tend to be negative, may improve your mood. Up or down, the change is likely to be temporary—and, to some degree, a result of how you perceive heart disease, either as a major setback or a second chance to live a healthier, happier, more meaningful life. Setbacks can leave us feeling vulnerable and unsure, while the thought of a second chance, fueled by gratitude and appreciation, can be energizing.

So where do you go from here? Here's where Pollyanna's "Glad Game" comes in. If you do nothing to change your attitude, the outlook you had prior to your cardiac event will prevail. If you decide that, for the sake of your heart, you want to maintain as much of a positive attitude as you can, you'll need to do some work. Norman Doidge, author of *The Brain That Changes Itself*, explains, "... as what is learned becomes a [bad] habit, it basically takes over a 'brain map' " and, "each time we repeat it, it claims more control of that map and prevents the use of that space for 'good' habits."

According to Doidge, the brain is not merely an "empty container" with learning a matter of "putting something in it." To create new habits (a way of thinking is a habit) repetition, correction and persistence are required. These new habits, or improved attitude, compete for space within the brain map, so the only way your long-held negative attitude will relinquish its domain is if you persist with creating new habits. Small changes, practiced regularly, can make a difference.

Here's what you can do: If your tendency is to automatically grumble and complain about life, begin each day listing five things that you're grateful for. If your habit is to judge others negatively, practice thinking something positive about each person you meet and every person you know. If your tendency is to predict that your day will go badly, think about something that will go well.

Being a Pollyanna doesn't mean you're fooling yourself. It means that even as you see the difficulties that come with life, you're training your brain to attend to the other side—the good side. Before your heart attack, before bypass surgery or your implanted stent you knew when your mood was straining your health. You knew but you thought you would stay healthy anyway. Make a change: thinking positively will change your life.

35

Finally, the scientific community is examining women's unique biological makeup and its impact on prevention, diagnosis and treatment of coronary artery disease. At a recent American Heart Association conference, the life-shortening effects of smoking, complications a woman may experience following implantation of defibrillators, hormone replacement therapy, and problems arising from long-term use of oral contraceptives were addressed.

According to Harvard Medical School's *The Healthy Heart: Preventing, Detecting, and Treating Coronary Artery Disease*, women with heart disease are 50% more likely to die from their illness than men. Within the crucial first year following a heart attack a woman is 38% more likely to die compared to her male counterpart, with a 25% risk of death. Explanations for these differences, according to *The Healthy Heart* are: age at time of diagnosis, the presence of coronary microvascular disease (a form of heart disease more difficult to detect using common diagnostic methods), inferior diagnosis and treatment, and a lack of clarity when it comes to the symptoms a woman might report.

What about male-female psychological differences? Discussions held in cardiac-support groups reveal dissimilar concerns. For women, a topic more popular than personal matters: feelings of stress stemming from worry about the physical and emotional needs of others. Women express an ongoing struggle with saying the word "no." Knowing that lack of assertion can lead to exhaustion and poor self-care doesn't make change any easier—the consequences attached to "no" are too risky. "No" can mean the end of a friendship or loss of image as caring or nice, which are biologically- and socially-driven identities. A woman's exaggerated sense of duty means relinquishing time she would have used to take an afternoon nap. Even after a life-threatening, life-altering heart attack women will abandon critically important cardiac-rehabilitation programs because time away from family means neglect. Guilt can be more painful than the pains of poor health.

This is not meant to encourage you to become hard-hearted, but to be realistic. Ask for help. Learn to say "no" and test your predictions: do you lose friends or do you gain respect? Avoid feeling guilty because you can't do it all. When in doubt, ask your heart, *Should I or should I not do this extra work?* Try to nap each day—even 20 minutes. Try to give yourself a half-hour of exercise each day. Carefully consider food choices. Doing these things may extend your life. There will be more time to devote yourself to those who you love. But for now ... today ... devote yourself to you.

36

In "You, Staying Young" (Roizen & Oz, 2007), stress is presented in categories: 1) daily stressful moments (a missed bus, a stain on your new outfit, being left on hold for a very long time); 2) failing to live in the present (chronic worry about all you have to do this afternoon, tomorrow, next week); and 3) acute, traumatic events (divorce, a new job, moving, losing a loved one).

Health outcomes following a "category 3" stressor that stunned the world were reported in the January 2008 issue of *Archives of General Psychiatry* (Holman, et al.). Investigators studying the after effects of acute stress associated with the 9/11 terrorist attacks reported a 53% increased incidence of cardiovascular ailments in the three years following this day in history.

Fortunately, there have been no further attacks. Still, scores of disturbing occurrences and worrisome "category 3" conditions mark our lives. Since that bright Tuesday morning we grieve for newly lost loved ones, marriages fail, millions are uprooted as homes fall to foreclosure, the list of the unemployed grows, too many of the 78 million baby boomers are financially unprepared, mothers and fathers mourn lost sons and daughters in Iraq and Afghanistan, and thousands are diagnosed with life-threatening illness. The heart carries it all.

If you've experienced an acute event, the way your body functions will tell the story of your ability to cope. Restless sleep, poor concentration, changes in appetite, bodily aches, irritability, excessive use of alcohol or drugs, feeling on edge, or a thickening midsection may be signs that adaptation is poor. You may need to take action now, before illness strikes or worsens.

There are a wide variety of stress-reducing methods. The one you choose should meet your personal needs: your schedule, budget, current level of health, flexibility and energy. It's best if what you do is transportable (you can carry dancing shoes with you wherever you go!). If what you do to lessen stress has an element of fun and playfulness (swimming, Ping-Pong, pottery), sticking with it will be easy. If it feels like work, if it bores you, you'll find a million reasons not to do it and eventually abandon it completely.

Taking charge of stress does not mean pretending that what has happened to you didn't. But it may mean that as you think of your disappointment, feel your sorrow, or struggle to get back on your feet, the positive steps you take will act as buffers to the damaging effects of stress so keenly felt by your heart.

What can you do about stress? Breathe slowly and deeply, meditate, cultivate a strong social network, share your home with a pet in need, get in the habit of taking afternoon naps, connect with nature, walk 30 minutes at least five days each week, reach out for help if you need it, and focus on what's right—not wrong. Life is short, don't make it shorter.

37

Depressed patients have been known to report feeling better the moment their physician hands them a prescription for an antidepressant—before they've taken a first dose. When asked why this might be, the reason given involves a return of hope. Current theory (Snyder, Rand, & Sigmon, 2002) expands the original definition of hope from "a perception that one's goals can be attained" to "one can find pathways to desired goals and become motivated to use those pathways." Maintaining or recovering health always involves setting goals and finding the necessary pathways to attain the desired outcome. A core element of depression—hopelessness— often triggers the thought, *No matter what I do, things won't get better,* reflecting chronic despair. A lack of drive is heard in, *I don't feel like exercising, so I won't.* Hope may drive motivation but action precedes motivation. Don't wait to feel like exercising before you take action. Exercise first. Hope and motivation will follow.

38

Famed turn-of-the-century psychologist William James referred to those so pessimistic that they believed "All natural goods perish; riches take wings; fame is a breath; love is a cheat; youth and health and pleasure will vanish." But he also referred to those who "flung themselves onto the goodness of life, in spite of their own hardships" as having "souls of a sky-blue tint." To live the life of a—probably healthier, according to studies—optimist, there is no requirement for constant bliss or endless happiness. Still, you can respond to difficulties with hope, have patience during a grueling stretch of life, and remind yourself every chance you get of what there is to be grateful for.

39

Researcher Robert Emmons (1999) created four categories classifying goals people tend to pursue: Intimacy, spirituality, generosity and power. All but one—power—predicted greater levels of subjective well-being.

Power was related to higher levels of negative mood. Power, described as a desire to influence and affect others (e.g., "Get others to see my point of view" or "Be the best when with a group of people"), may mimic the social needs of primates repeatedly reestablishing dominance within the confines of ever-changing social groupings. For the primates, this need for dominance, or power, is associated with greater cardiovascular arousal and subsequently, greater coronary artery disease. Once again, common sense suggests that thinking outside of ourselves, being willing to connect with others and transcending the self with some form of spirituality, and thinking about what it is we might contribute to society can be linked to a greater sense of well-being and, most important, a healthy heart.

40

If you've been diagnosed with heart disease you've probably been asked again and again how your body feels: Any discomfort?" "Do you experience recurring pain? Shortness of breath? Fatigue? How about your medication—any unusual reactions?

Since your diagnosis, has anyone asked you how you feel emotionally? Here's why they should: More frequent or intense negative emotional responses can happen after a cardiac event. It might be assumed that, as recovery proceeds, troubling feelings, for example, worry about loss of energy, or about being able to return to work, or having a second heart attack, decrease as confidence and optimism return. But new studies suggest this may not be true.

Most medical experts recognize that it isn't unusual for patients to leave the hospital after having coronary artery bypass surgery feeling in control and upbeat, but then feel helpless and sad in the weeks ahead. These negative emotions are expected to remit—and usually do—as a patient's physical stamina is restored. But new research indicates that there's potential for negative emotions to continue and increase, which puts a heart patient at greater risk of further complications.

A recently completed study at Massachusetts's Lown Cardiovascular Research Foundation, in which patients were followed for more than three years after a cardiac event, found that patients' levels of anxiety regarded as "normal" at baseline did not indicate what levels of anxiety would be in the months and years following diagnosis.

The lead investigator of the Lown study, Dr. Woldecherkos Shibeshi, reported "increasing and persistent anxiety" (increased during the 3½-year period) to be associated with doubling the risk of heart attack or death. Again, the level of anxiety measured at the start of the study had little predictive value. Participants who felt fearful immediately following a cardiac event who managed to cope with anxiety effectively during the three-year follow-up period had better medical outcomes than those whose anxiety was either high or low in the beginning, but increased over time.

If you worry excessively, feel apprehensive and irritable, have tense muscles and poor sleep, you might be anxious. Because of its complexity, the treatment for anxiety isn't one size fits all. The skills and techniques you use to manage anxiety should be specific, targeting and modifying your particular worries and fears. For example, thoughts associated with generalized anxiety may require a different emphasis of care than the thoughts associated with obsessive-compulsive disorder or panic attacks.

Whatever the form, if you have heart disease—even if it's been a year or more since you've had a cardiac event—excessive and persistent arousal resulting from anxiety may lead to more complications. If you're increasingly anxious, if you're more worried and unsure than you were when your heart problems started, it's time to talk with your doctor.

41

Largely, material about women's vulnerability to heart disease provided by the scientific and medical communities and media centers focuses on the familiar topics of exercise, weight, eating properly, avoiding smoking, maintaining a healthy blood pressure, controlling cholesterol and triglycerides, and getting tested for diabetes. Only occasionally and often superficially do we hear about women and stress. What triggers stress in a woman's life and how she responds may stem from differences in biology, societal expectations and a woman's instinct to nurture.

But the word is getting out.

The American Heart Association's "Red Dress" campaign symbolizes the need for greater awareness of the historically inferior levels of care afforded women at risk for cardiac illness. Using a grassroots approach, on one day each February the Heart Association encourages all women to wear red clothing—or a red dress lapel pin from the association—as a way to bring attention to the severity and pervasiveness of the problem.

Perhaps it should be a red hat, to remind everyone just how many hats women wear. Women are responsible for too many roles, causing stress levels to rise, adding to the likelihood of developing heart disease.

Women are mothers caring for active, young children. They're mothers to grown children returning home from a failed career or marriage. They're daughters attending to ageing, frail, sometimes troubled parents. They're employers and employees while simultaneously managing all the duties of full-time housekeeper. Women are chauffeurs, cooks, gardeners. They're wives struggling to keep a marriage together. They're the dog walker, savvy shopper, night-duty nurse, psychological counselor for friends, and business consultants and administrative assistants to their husbands. Women are money managers and financial consultants. Women are construction contractors when the roof leaks and kindling gatherers when the winds blow cold.

There's never time to do it all. A busy, frantic heart is a stressed heart. Women do their best to keep up and, most of the time, do it all with a smile. The smile is meant to help them look better than they feel and to reassure those they care about that everything is OK, even when it's not.

Women get exhausted. When women are stressed they eat more than they should and make poor food choices, usually the easiest-to-find, most accessible snacks they can get their hands on. Women smoke to calm frayed nerves. They turn to alcohol to slow a racing mind. Women don't find time to exercise. Women forget to take their vitamins. They don't have time to get a checkup. Women get heart disease more often than men. Women with heart disease die more often than men.

Here's what you can do:

- Breathe in slowly through your nose 10 times in the morning, 10 times at night and when you think of it during the day.
- Take 30 minutes out of each day to walk.
- Cut your daily task list.
- Ask for help.
- Say "no" more often.
- Stay in the present: A mind always reaching for the next item on the to-do list is a stressed mind.
- Learn how to meditate.
- Realize your limitations. Accept the fact that you don't have to do it all. Realize that if you were gone tomorrow, the people who seem to need you more often than they should would somehow manage. Stop thinking that you have to control everything. Let it be. The world won't fall apart.
- Take time today to live fully for yourself and for those you love.

42

Depression is a serious matter. It may contribute to the development of heart disease. It may lead to medical complications following a heart attack or coronary artery bypass surgery.

Cognitive-behavioral treatment is highly effective for the treatment of depression, equally as effective as antidepressant medication. In fact, many scientists and physicians believe that therapy and medication combined promise the best possible outcome. If depression is in some way causative when it comes to the progression of heart disease, or interfering when it comes to recovery, we would expect that successful treatment for depression would lead to a reduction in complications and recurrences of cardiac events, impacting positively on survival rates. To date, there are no studies suggesting that it makes a difference. A few possible explanations for this mystery:

- Waiting too long before seeking treatment may mean limitations on what can be accomplished medically once severe vascular damage has occurred.
- If time spent in therapy is too short, as may be the case in most research trials, there may be little, if any, real cognitive change. In a matter of weeks a solid understanding of unhealthy, negative thought patterns can be acquired. But lasting change occurs over time with mindful effort, repetition and experimentation in the rather short time period afforded most studies, change may be minimal and fragile.
- A reduction in the frequency and intensity of negative feelings doesn't necessarily mean an increase in heart-protective positive feelings. If what is achieved in treatment for depression means no longer crying, no longer feeling sad and no longer feeling irritable, it may not be enough. Perhaps improvement starts when we begin to experience joy, when we're able to laugh, when we see ourselves engaged in things we really like to do, when life feels full and rewarding and we at last know what people mean when they use the term "well-being."

If you think you're depressed, get help. Don't wait until after a diagnosis of heart disease. The longer you wait the more complicated and dangerous things become.

43

If you've experienced a major loss or trauma or setback in your life you may find yourself searching for answers. The search for understanding helps us cope; it makes us feel that we have some amount of control over the troubling matter. The result is that we may wake up one morning feeling a new zest for life. The information, knowledge and understanding you gain may contribute to the development of personal strengths such as inspiration, interest, curiosity, acceptance—even courage.

So when things are tough, what do you do? Begin your search. Acknowledging your strengths, exercising your character, your virtues and your values, means your heart wants to live, wants to flourish, wants to go on.

44

When the unexpected happens—something hurtful or painful or alarming—you might think, *I don't understand ... how could this happen ... why did this happen*? If we can figure out the how and the why, we hold onto the belief that we're in charge and in control. It's too unsettling to accept the notion that life is comprised of random happenings—events we can't predict and circumstances out of our hands. So we review the details: *If I had just done this instead of that, this wouldn't have happened.* If we can master the unplanned we'll avoid feeling bewildered and vulnerable in the future.

When you believe you've done what you were supposed to do but you had a heart attack anyway, control flies out the window. You review the checklist of things that seemed to be in order: your weight was normal; cholesterol was under control; you didn't have hypertension; you stopped smoking years ago; you exercised regularly. You're OK now, you made it through the attack, but what went wrong? Will you ever feel confident again? Was all the effort a waste of time?

Nothing was wasted. Without the effort, the heart attack may have killed you. Because of all that exercise you did and the fish you ate and stress you learned to manage, your recovery may be faster and more complete. Because of the way you took care of your health, you may need lower doses of prescribed medications.

As children we ask, "Why do birds fly?" or "Why is the sky blue?" These are questions that might be easier to answer than, *Why did my health fail when I did everything right?* Answers or not, your goals should be the same: controlling your weight, exercising regularly, managing negative emotions, eating a healthful diet, learning to adapt to the unexpected and learning to cope with unknowns. All of these will add to the likelihood of a long, well-lived, healthy life—in spite of a heart attack, in spite of anything. Maybe you can live without an answer to every question.

45

Nansook Park, Christopher Peterson and Martin Seligman (2006), three leading authorities in the field of positive psychology, conducted an investigation of the populations of 54 nations with the goal of seeing how similar or dissimilar they may be in their commitment to personal strengths. In the United States the most commonly expressed strengths were kindness, fairness, honesty, gratitude and judgment. Since being grateful fosters optimism, and both gratitude and optimism are related to health and well-being, this is a good thing. The least identified were prudence, modesty and self-regulation.

Placing less importance on self-regulation is not a good thing. When we eat too much, smoke or push ourselves past the point of fatigue, regulation is replaced with denial. If the approximately 85,000 US study participants didn't view themselves as valuing control, then the obesity epidemic shouldn't be a surprise. Nor should the hundreds of thousands who die each year from heart disease. Or the rapidly growing number of diabetics losing limbs and lives.

The five most valued strengths are said to reflect "universal values for a viable society." They're ultimately what make survival possible. If we fail to embrace the least valued strengths of prudence, modesty and self-regulation, society won't suffer—society will continue just fine without us. It's individuals and those who love them who suffer.

Take the first step: Ask yourself what it is you truly value. How much importance do you place on eating well, being healthy, feeling energetic and getting enough exercise? The way you feel and the health of your heart is a result of thousands of small choices made day after day—choices that reflect what you care about most. If you had to choose between good health, independence and vitality or another piece of pizza or a donut, which would it be? With every choice you make today take a breath, wait 30 seconds, then decide.

46

If lately you've been feeling blue, you may be depressed. Health practitioners determine types and severity of clinical depression with the help of a diagnostic manual created to improve the accuracy of their observations. The greater the number of matching symptoms between the text and the client, the greater the diagnostic certainty. Without a doubt, manuals are useful: They offer caregivers a common language and help to increase confidence in treatment choices. However, people's emotions don't always fall into a manual's clear and absolute guidelines. With one symptom, such as feeling sad, you would fall far short of what's required to indicate clinical depression, but that doesn't mean you should ignore how you feel. Chronic sadness by itself may have a significant, negative impact on the health of your heart.

Sadness interferes with motivation. You might glance at your bottle of blood pressure medication and not feel like taking it. Maybe you put off making a follow-up visit to the doctor. Exercise seems like too much effort. You notice that you're waking up several times in the night. The first thing you think about each morning is how tired you feel. You can't see that your immune system isn't up to par, but you feel run down. You can't feel inflammation, but it's there.

One of the first things your doctor may ask you to do is be more active. If you've been dragging around, barely able to do what you need to do, you might exit the doctor's office feeling misunderstood. But your doctor has just given you the best possible prescription—movement. You don't have to feel like doing something to do it: Taking a walk requires legwork, not feeling work.

Start small. Walk for five minutes. If it's hard to get outside, make a list of activities you can do at home. Stretch, call a friend, sketch the tree you see as you look out your window. Clean out your briefcase or purse, or polish your shoes. Ride your stationary bike for three minutes (if you can safely get on and off). Visit a museum, rake leaves, trim a tree. Move. Action is one of the fastest and most reliable ways to lift mood. With action comes motivation and with motivation comes hope.

47

Even when we know exactly how to improve our health, doing it isn't always easy. Scientists Kennon Sheldon and Sonja Lyubomirsky remind us that effort is "needed to initiate activity" and certainly needed to "carry out and maintain activity," and in a 2004 study suggest that we're more likely to follow through with activities—including ones that are good for us—when they're compatible with who we are and when they suit our personality. If our actions are accompanied by the way we perceive them, it makes sense that someone who considers going to the gym a boring chore but a run outside as a freeing experience, is more likely to skip the gym and head outside for a run. If an exercise or activity is believed to be boring, it'll be a struggle—it'll always be an effort. So what suits you? Pick a heart-healthy activity that you enjoy. What satisfies your appreciation of beauty or interest in exploration? Is it hiking, gardening, walking your dog, swimming, playing golf—without a cart? Exercise doesn't only have to happen in a gym.

48

One of my heart patients reported that following his heart attack he felt fear rather than calm as he walked alone on the beach. In the past, the feeling of warm sand underfoot, the blue sky above and the familiar smell of the ocean he loved brought him feelings of renewal. Now such walks were overwhelmed with self-doubt and worry. He'd think, *What if I suddenly need help? What if something happens to my heart? What would I do?*

After a cardiac event, perhaps it's not a good idea to venture out to remote places without a companion until you feel emotionally and physically confident. However, if you eliminate visits with nature entirely, you may miss out on the recuperative benefits of natural settings. Viewing natural scenes such as a sandy shoreline, waterfall or mountain vista, improves mood, reducing the risk of further medical complications.

You're less likely to be anxious when you're immersed in something you enjoy or appreciate. Observing nature impacts the nervous system, resulting in lowered heart rate and blood pressure and reduced muscle tension. So stroll through the park, walk along a country road and, if you're stuck at work, gaze out a window. For one week record how much time you spend noticing or enjoying the natural world around you. Then next week double it if you can. Your heart will feel the healing.

49

Introducing new cage mates into a primate environment leads to social instability—and coronary artery disease. Sensing threat, older group members experience chronic stress as they struggle to reestablish positions of dominance.

We are primates. When we feel unsure we choose to impress others with status and dominance. The more we try to impress, the less worthy we feel. This struggle to impress is born out of insecurity, and insecurity corresponds with high arousal, constriction of blood vessels, increased blood pressure and higher levels of circulating cholesterol.

What's more important: impressing people with how great you are or living with a healthy heart?

50

It's unlikely that the experiences of any two cardiac patients will be exactly alike. Unique perceptions of the same event will foster unlimited combinations of feelings and behaviors. Still, there are common human themes in strength of character or virtue that help us to "endure tough situations" (Rate, et al., 2007). Courage is one of those virtues and if we take notice, we see it expressed over and over again by both the fearful and the confident.

We have one heart. We depend on this heart to beat continuously, hour after hour, for decades and decades. There is no back-up muscle, no left or right heart. Only one. If you've been diagnosed with heart disease, the reality of what has happened might be a shock. With such reality some respond with fear and self-doubt, focusing on the unfamiliar, unpredictable nature of heart disease, while others feel more confident, determined and eager to reestablish personal control. Still others respond with anger, regret and frustration.
Most of us think of courage as that moment when an individual selflessly puts her life on the line to save another, even a stranger. Someone coming forth willingly at great personal risk to reveal a truth for the good of others might be labeled courageous.

Based on the input gathered from participants in Rate's study, the characteristics of a truly courageous or "ideal" person broaden.

Following a heart attack, bypass surgery or any challenge to the function or structure of the heart, a heart patient can be defined in the following quote: "Courage, also called fortitude or bravery, is the ability to endure what is necessary to achieve a good end; even in the face of great obstacles" (Cavanagh & Moberg, 1999, cited in Clarke, et al., 2007). It can be observed in the following actions:

- Can handle and remains composed in tough situations.
- Perseveres in the face of obstacles and under pressure.
- Does not quit when the going gets tough.
- Does not back down when scared.
- Fights through pain and pressure.
- Does not give up.
- Accomplishes something despite personal fear.

51

Work on filtering out negative information in your life. Are you listening to the news too often? Do you notice how you feel when you do? Plan to filter in positive information. Rent a funny movie or listen to calming music. If you know someone who complains too often, pay attention to whether or not you may be reinforcing his negative talk. Are you too available? Do you spend a great deal of time trying to help this person solve his problems? Negative thinking and negative feelings may trigger the release of stress hormones that are hard on the heart. Laughter increases blood flow to the heart by a healthy 22%.

52

What really makes us happy? Behavioral scientists Kennon Sheldon and Sonja Lyubomirsky have developed a straightforward model of happiness that not only answers that question but also tells us how do go about achieving even more of it.

A fairly constant, inherited set point (what we're born with) accounts for about half of our good humor. Life circumstances such as age, marital status and income account for just 10% of those sought-after good feelings, while the remaining 40% is all about what we choose to think and do.

Note the word "choose," meant to reflect what these scientists refer to as "intentional activity." It seems the happiest among us look on the brighter side of even the most disturbing challenges. These people regularly engage in positive behaviors like exercising, practicing generosity and kindness toward others, and being appreciative. Pursuing even the simplest goals that really mean something stimulate feelings associated with happiness, such as enthusiasm, curiosity and a sense of purpose.

So do most of us have it backwards? We probably spend 40% of our time pursuing what ultimately offers 10% of our happy feelings and only 10% of our time pursuing what is likely to offer about 40% of true joy and satisfaction.

How often have your heard someone say, "If I could lose 20 pounds I'd be happy!" or "When I get that raise I'll be a happy person" or "How do you expect me to be happy when I don't have a mate?" Here's a rewrite: "I'll take a bit of my grocery money and give it to the food bank." (Less food and lower weight equal higher happiness level due to generosity.) Or "I'm so grateful to be working during these difficult times." (Better feelings translate into better work effort and a greater chance of improved earning, plus appreciation brings good mood, and good mood brings positive recognition.) Or "It will be a whole lot easier for me to find a mate if I'm in a good frame of mind." (Smiling, pleasant people are simply more attractive.)

Momentary happiness may be found inside a box of chocolates or with a new mobile phone or new outfit, but reliable happiness is the byproduct of the positive things we do again, again and again.

53

Perception is everything. One simple word can carry more than its precise meaning. For example, according to a dictionary the word "flower" means "the part of a plant from which the fruit or seed is developed." But to you, "flower" might mean garden or romance or funeral. Whatever the word means to you will influence the way you feel when you hear it.

What about words used by your doctor, nurse, medical laboratory or insurance company? How do those words make you feel?

Describing illness, pharmaceutical firms rely on "medicalized" terms. Rather than high blood pressure they use the word hypertension. Insurance companies demand "medical necessity" when deciding whether or not you'll be reimbursed for health-care expenses. To pass the necessity test, a physician will describe your symptoms using the most medicalized language that can be reasonably applied to your particular illness.

Would you rather be told you have gastro esophageal reflux disease or heartburn?

The journal *Public Library of Science One* (cited in sciencedaily, 2008) reports that when presented with names of medical disorders using either lay or medicalized terms, participants responded to conditions described with less familiar language as more serious, disease-like and rare. The result? More worry and the potential for a negative effect on self-care.

Attitude has so much to do with recovery, and fear and worry don't promote a good one. Optimism, however, supports the best kind of thinking: you will recover, what you have is fairly common, others do well with treatment and, if you take care of yourself, you too will do just as well. When words frighten or confuse you, ask your physician to describe your illness using clear, easily understood words. Ask: How serious is this? What can I expect? Can I exercise?

How might I feel in the coming weeks and months? What does my future hold?

As medical knowledge grows, so will the mysterious words used to describe it. Words have power, but most of the power comes from the way we process what we hear. If you walk out of your doctor's office feeling worried and unsure, go back and ask more questions. Knowing exactly what you're facing is the first step in knowing how to proceed and take care of yourself.

54

We hear again and again how adversity contributes to the development of resilience and personal growth. While that's true, it's also true that when adversity persists over time with little or no improvement in conditions of health or environment, individuals may begin to feel weakened, unable to rise above their burdens. We can't predict when a threshold is reached. We can't say exactly when the difficulties of life stop being character builders and instead contribute to a deterioration of health. Everyone has a tipping point. When no matter how hard you try and nothing seems to help, feelings of helplessness and despair set the stage for the development of inflammation, turbulent blood flow and poor immune function. Listen to your body. If the stressful conditions of your life have continued for too long, pay attention to how you're feeling. If you have more aches and pains than usual, if you always feel as if you're coming down with a cold, if minor wounds don't heal as quickly as they should, if you're irritable, or your sleep patterns or appetite have changed, these may be signs of emotional and physical overload. You may have depression. It's imperative that you discuss your symptoms with your general practitioner or cardiologist. Hearing your health-care provider name what it is you're feeling may be the first step toward lifting this burden, clearing the path for growth and newfound resilience.

55

Whether it's a computer download, an order being shipped, a home-delivered meal, a return on an investment, a trip in the car or a promised phone call—we're so impatient, we want everything now! With the latest technology our questions are answered in seconds. We eat fast food more than we eat healthful food. Our hairdresser gets us in and get us out. Our dry cleaning can be ready in an hour and, with the right GPS in our car, we'll never again have to wait in traffic.

Let's not lose our appreciation for time. Time is good. Crops depend on it for growth. Children require it for development. Over time friendships deepen. With time comes wisdom. There is no substitute for the passing of time. In fact, sometimes letting it pass can help us find exactly what you're searching for.

With time we find solutions that come as our minds incubate. That might mean during the seven or eight hours we allot to a night's sleep. According to a May 2007 *New York Times* article, "Sleep appears to play a role in helping people make big picture realizations." In the article Dr. Jeffrey Ellenbogen, of Brigham and Women's Hospital, in Boston, reports that during sleep "brains may be sorting out information … making connections that can lead to new insights."

When you're wrestling with a problem, let a little time go by. Describe your dilemma, write it down then put it away for a day. Let your resting mind do the work. An added benefit: a rested heart beats longer.

56

Maybe your hard-driving, competitive friend has less of a chance of having a heart attack than the one who is socially ill at ease—the one who stays home complaining all the time about how bad things are.

Withdrawing, fearing rejection, feeling inadequate and irritable much of the time may be signs of depression or an avoidant personality or both. Within cardiac literature people fitting this description are referred to as Type D. Until the last decade we've believed that the aggressive Type A was the most likely candidate for developing heart disease. That's not necessarily the case. When social anxiety keeps you away from people, the protective benefits of human contact are missed. Surprisingly, after a heart attack, even when recovery appears to be going well, loneliness and isolation may increase the risk of death. If an opportunity presents itself for a new activity and you decide to stay home, not only do you feel more alone, but you miss the valuable information people share when they get together. For example, someone you meet in a support group might give you the name of a great cardiologist.

It's easier to complain when we're alone. We have no opposing voice, no one to offer the other side of the story. The worse we feel, the less we do. In the meantime, the Type A runs enthusiastically to the first cardiac-rehabilitation program he can find. He takes advantage of anything and everything promising optimal health and a speedy recovery.

If you're a Type D, you don't have to become a Type A. But do take advantage of available support. You may never become an optimist, but make an effort to replace damaging negative thoughts with thoughts of appreciation. You may never become socially confident, but make an effort to be with others and when you do, tell yourself it's OK to feel uncomfortable.

Rather than focusing inward, focus outward toward the people you're with. Plan to complain as much as you like for one hour each day. For the other 23 hours, when a complaint comes to mind, tell yourself it's to be thought about at the appointed hour and only then. When all is said and done, be a Type Y: You, the one in charge of your health.

57

People say they feel "fragmented": The dining room table is not for eating—it's a place for junk mail and past-due bills. Your job isn't a place where you satisfy your need for a life of purpose—it's where you spend time thinking about whether or not you'll be made redundant. Managing money is less about emulating the prudent habits of Benjamin Franklin and more about needing a PhD in economics or a fortune-teller. With that, your doctor reminds you to eat well, avoid stress and stay as fit as possible with regular exercise and plenty of rest. Whew!

The more pressed for time we are, the smaller the percentage of effort we allot to each task. Feelings of accomplishment are replaced with feelings of guilt. We emphasize quantity as quality of life fades. That fragmented feeling tells us that with so many responsibilities, there's little we do with full attention and dedication. Meaning slips away.

When all organs and systems are functioning at their best, the body is said to be in a state of physiological coherence. You get a feeling of that from time to time—it's a feeling of well-being. On the other hand, when we're feeling fragmented, we feel separated from ourselves, broken and unsystematic. How can we put the pieces back together again?

Return to quality. Pay attention to what is beautiful around you and make things more beautiful when you get the chance. Use your finest china, even if it's only one plate you've been saving for a special time. Notice—really notice—the color of your spouse's eyes. Avoid measuring the success of each day by how many tasks you've completed and instead count the number of new words you've learned or the number of birds perched at your window. Notice your breath. Appreciate—really appreciate—something you've taken for granted. Listen—really listen—to the sound of the strings in the music you hear.

Be gentle with yourself and with those more vulnerable than you.

58

When heart disease strikes you, do everything you can to raise your chances for a best possible recovery. Take the medicine your physician has prescribed; exercise, also as prescribed; stay away from cigarettes; and don't overdo red meat. You think about this every day. You do your best. But there's more.

Have you considered how brave you are? You have a serious illness and, in spite of that, you're dauntless. You don't simply endure the challenge, you stand up and defiantly face the doubt—you keep going.

You haven't lost your sense of humor. You laugh at yourself. You tell your spouse a funny story. You joke with the doctor. You smile when your dog smiles at you.

And you're kind. No matter how scared you may have felt when you woke up in the hospital after your heart attack, you thanked the nurse who looked in on you. You tried to carry your belongings so your wife wouldn't have to. You sent a thank-you note to the EMS team that saved your life.

Recovery is in the character.

59

For the millions of people treated for depression there are just as many who receive no help at all. Why?

- A shortage of practitioners trained in problems of the mind.
- Some insurance policies, with an outdated view of the mind

and body being separate, don't include mental health services.
- There's a continuing stigma attached to a diagnosis of depression.
- Those who either don't identify their depression or, if they do, accept it as just the way things are.

When your cardiologist asks you how you feel it's easy enough to say, "I've been having trouble walking up stairs" or "I'm feeling more tired than usual" or "I've noticed a little dizziness." But if you've been feeling sad, worried or irritable, you might keep that to yourself. Perhaps you'll worry about what people will think, that there will be consequences if your boss finds out. Maybe you'll tell yourself, *I'm not weak—I can handle it.* So, to the question about emotions, you say to your doctor, "Oh, fine. Just fine. Thanks for asking."

Do you think if you lower your blood pressure, open your arteries and strengthen your heart the job is done? These improvements won't hold up if you neglect your mood. It is optimism that supports better habits. It is enthusiasm that keeps you moving. It is contentment that allows your body to relax. It is interest that makes the day worthwhile.

60

Your body's effort to maintain a balanced state, or stasis, is constant and predictable. For example, with every changing demand, blood pressure fluctuates, all day, all night. The same requirement for equilibrium applies to levels of water, nutrients, temperature and energy—all systems work when they find the right balance.

Regulation of the cardiovascular system has two routes: the sympathetic, triggering a rise in heart rate (needed when you ride your bicycle), and the parasympathetic, responsible for its slowing (when you digest a meal).

You probably haven't recently engaged in a lively discussion about heart rate regulation, but it's an important indicator of health. Researchers in India have found that you can actually influence control over your heart rate, developing a more stable heart rhythm. More stability means less wear-and-tear inside artery walls, less risk of developing inflammation and more even blood flow.

How can you find this balance that is so good for you? Yoga. Not a pill, not a procedure.

61

I can't relax.
I have so much to do—I'll never get it all done.
I'm not the type to relax. I have to be doing something all the time.

Really?

Try this:

Find a meditation or relaxation program that can be listened to on your iPod or CD player. For one hour, three days this week, listen to the program. Each day keep track of what you've accomplished. Was there a loss of productivity on the listening days? Could you do this again next week?

A rested heart will be there when you need it. Don't go through life chasing the next task. We never finish it all, anyway. Really.

62

Just last week one of my patients who I had not seen in months told me his primary care physician had given him a prescription for an antidepressant. I asked him what it was that seemed troubling. He said his boss had asked if, after more than 30 years of service, he had thought about when he might retire. In the employee's mind retirement was three or four years away. For the boss it was "any time soon."

As I drove home that evening, reviewing the day, I felt pleased that the doctor had made such a decision. This man was despondent—not a good emotional state for anyone, but worse for someone with a history of heart disease.

The medication will help lessen the potency of symptoms—sadness, poor sleep and difficulty making decisions. But what it won't do is erase the reality of a premature retirement. When the realization of what had happened sunk in, the patient saw himself transformed from a vigorous, contributing person, to a "useless"—as he referred to himself—aging man with little to offer.

Life does not end at retirement. There is still much to do. You are more than your job. Learn. Challenge yourself. Do all you can to find the opportunity in this experience. The plan you had was a good one; however, it's not necessarily the only one. Life has options. Go to your favorite spots—a best-loved chair, the beach, woods, a country road or the park in the middle of the city—and exercise your imagination.

There's no way to avoid loss. What you do with it is what makes the difference. All beginnings follow an ending.

63

An effective mood lifting exercise is the Three Good Things or Three Blessings technique: daily, for a period of two to three weeks, list three things that went well and why they went well.

Seems simple, right? Recently I spoke to a couple who found themselves complaining, failing to listen to each other, expecting the worst, fully prepared to battle that worst whenever they saw it coming. Although the Three Good Things exercise is generally done by one person, I thought it might be helpful if this couple did it together, moving their thinking in a positive direction. Here's how it went:

Something that went well: The woman had driven that day (usually avoided due to lack of confidence).

Why did it go well?
1. "Because we didn't crash."
2. "Because we didn't get lost."
3. "Because we didn't run out of gas."

Their thinking focused on the bad things that didn't happen! No wonder they were so dismal. Negativity had become their norm.

Hearing their words husband and wife began to laugh—at themselves. I asked them to try again.

Why did it go well?
1. "Because I got out there and gave it my best in spite of my fear."
2. "Because traffic was light."
3. "Because it was a beautiful day."

They called a week later to tell me how powerful this exercise had been, lifting their moods and improving the way each saw the other.

Such a small shift in attention, but what a difference it makes.

64

Perhaps you grew up hearing your parents tell you how smart, beautiful, talented and special you are. Or you didn't get much attention at all, in spite of all your remarkable qualities. Either way, in order to continue receiving compliments or satisfy a need for what you didn't get, you find yourself looking outward, hoping others will see how special you are. When feedback is positive, mood will be the same, but even a small amount of criticism leaves you feeling dejected and dark.

Does it surprise you to learn that people with this emotional makeup are more likely to develop heart disease? Any unmet need for recognition or admiration feels like a threat, so the heart beats hard. Frustration comes when a partner finds it impossible to meet the insatiable need for attention this person craves, so blood vessels constrict. Loneliness comes when no one seems to understand, so self-care seems pointless.

The rhythm of the heart goes well when we find ways to cooperate, when we consider the impact of our words and deeds on those we meet, when we let go of the need to impress, when we see true beauty and uniqueness in the simple and ordinary.

Free yourself. You need air, water and food. You don't need approval.

65

Panic disorder is a form of anxiety diagnosed more by thoughts reported than by symptoms. For example, people will say that at the time of heightened anxiety they think, *I'm going to faint, I can't breathe, I'll suffocate, I'll be trapped and won't be able to get out, I'll lose my mind.*

The sufferer is convinced that he has a serious, life-threatening ailment. One woman with chronic chest pain believed she had heart disease. She was cleared medically, then began thinking her doctors had missed the diagnosis and it was only a matter of time before she would have a heart attack. That was 30 years ago. Today she still doesn't have heart disease and, now that she's sought treatment, doesn't have panic.

Fears associated with panic disorder are generally no more than that—fears. Nevertheless, we know that overuse of the nervous system associated with intense, negative emotion, can be hard on the cardiovascular system.

Dr. Kate Walters, of University College London, says the relationship between panic disorder and heart disease is not fully understood. It may be that what is initially diagnosed as panic is heart disease, or that heart disease comes as a result of anxiety.

Chronic arousal may contribute to a process of clogging arteries or unhealthy changes in heart rate.

What should you do if you suffer from panic?

First, have a complete physical. If you're told you have no signs of illness, but you continue to have panic attacks or you fear having one, it's time to get help. In therapy (preferably cognitive-behavioral therapy) you'll learn to observe symptoms, reframing them as cues to mentally direct yourself toward feeling calm and safe.

With treatment, patients usually begin to feel better quickly. By learning that not what you believe is happening at the time of a panic attack, but what is truly happening is an important part of recovery. Changing your belief from, *I feel dizzy—I'm going to faint in public to I never faint when I feel this way—I'm feeling dizzy because my breathing is shallow … let me breathe deeply* will bring you to a new level of confidence.

Remember, if you trick your body into believing you are in danger, your body will do all it can to protect you. Your heart will pump hard, blood pressure will rise, breath will grow shallow and you'll have a strong desire to flee. Your body will never challenge you on this danger, whether it's real or imagined. It will believe what you say and respond accordingly.

66

Perhaps you've discovered your best qualities during this time of adversity—as you recover from cardiac surgery or struggle to absorb the reality of having had a heart attack.

Perhaps what matters most and who matters most has never been so clear.

You promise you'll never waste a day. The next time someone says something foolish, you'll let it go. You know you'll take time each day to speak with someone you love, and really listen to what they say. When you walk your dog you'll leave your cell phone at home. You'll ask the man at the newsstand how he's feeling and wait for him to answer before scanning the morning headlines. You'll hold back the urge to impress anyone with how much you know.

67

Is there room for gratitude if your heart is failing?

Maybe you don't think so. You think you don't deserve this fatigue, this breathlessness, this loss of interest in things you've always loved to do, this awareness of the limits of time. You're sad. Sometimes you're angry.

No matter how bleak the day, gratitude has a way of shifting attention from what seems to be missing to what we've been given. In a grateful moment you see what you may otherwise ignore: the outstretched hand of a small child, the green of spring grass, a best friend's smile, the stranger who went out of her way to show kindness.

When hope is dim, more than ever you need something to help you cope. Try gratitude. It may surprise you.

68

At least two to three times each week someone tells me how much happier he or she would be if so and so would behave differently. This is usually accompanied with a vague, *Of course, I know it's not all him or her, but* … Then the patient continues telling me how someone else's way of behaving is interfering with his or her ability to have a positive outlook.

It's not the way others behave, it's the way you think. If you make other people responsible for your happiness, your reactions will be unruly.

- Your mate doesn't take out the garbage. You're unhappy.
- Your best friend is late again and you've waiting in the coffee shop for 10 extra minutes. You're frustrated.
- Your co-worker didn't respond to the message you sent yesterday. You're insulted.
- You start thinking how inconsiderate everyone is, how completely undependable. They're ruining your life and your mood.

Was it the trash, the 10 minutes, the delayed reply or was it that you turned these events into something intolerable, something more important than they should be?

Your thoughts, your mood. Yours, not theirs.

69

In the critical first year following a heart attack so many questions are swirling in your mind. When will I be able to return to my routine? What's a safe level or amount of exercise? I'm feeling better—must I continue taking this medication? Can I eat a hamburger once in a while? What about going back to work? Should I go back? Do I want to?

Generally, your primary care physician, cardiologist and cardiac rehabilitation staff will have the answers you need. Of course, doubts about employment may be more difficult to resolve than questions about hamburgers.

We define ourselves by what we do. Work means a certain place to go at a certain time, certain days of the week. More than a paycheck, going to work means routine and familiarity. But now you've had a heart attack. Suddenly life is more than what you do—the workplace may not hold the same attraction that it once had.

In one scientific study it was found that people returning to highly demanding work settings were at greater risk of future cardiac events, including second heart attacks, when their position didn't provide much in the way of decision-making ability. Having a great deal of responsibility but little control is stressful for your heart.

A hard-driving CEO may have a lower risk for heart disease (high demand, high control position) than his middle managers (high demand, low control). The employee with the least amount of responsibility and least amount of control (low demand, low control) may also be protected and less likely to suffer the consequences of job strain.

Do you need to define your position as low or high on the demand scale before making a decision about whether it's best to return to your job? Maybe it's enough to see how mentally and physically spent you feel each evening when you return home. What about those edgy feelings you have each Sunday, knowing where you'll be and what you'll be doing on Monday? How about mornings? Enthusiasm or dread?

This doesn't mean you should not work, but where you work, what you do and how you feel about it matters. As you make a decision, don't just ask your doctor, ask your heart.

70

There is a saying, "You have the face you deserve by the time you reach 50." (Translation: years of having a positive or negative attitude will be visible to the naked eye, written all over your face.)

If life has treated you kindly, if you tend to see positive elements in the most troubling events, if you feel good about the people you know the warmth you feel inside is likely to shine through. If, on the other hand, you feel removed from others, if you feel distant and cheerless, feelings of loneliness may be the language of your expression. What would the inner workings of the body of a lonely person reveal? Adverse effects of stress hormones accumulate, leaving in their wake the telltale signs of declining health.

Research brings greater clarity to the topic of loneliness and helps us understand more about the relationship between isolation and heart disease. Lonely individuals are found to have higher levels of circulating epinephrine that would encourage chronic activation of the fight or flight response. This means elevated blood pressure, increased cardiac output, heightened vigilance (scanning the environment for threat), changes in blood platelets—all which increase the possibility of clotting. Younger lonely individuals suffer from poor sleep, limiting the amount of restoration and repair needed for a healthy mind and body.

On the surface it would seem the answer to loneliness is to reach out, join something, help others and find new friends. These are all good ideas, but loneliness is complicated. For example, it's possible to continue feeling lonely in the presence of others. Perception matters more than circumstance. For some, loneliness may be tied to heredity. For others, it is linked to poor social skills, low self-esteem and fear of rejection.

Whatever the cause, if you suffer from ongoing loneliness, it is a good idea to meet with a counselor. If that's not possible, join a support group for persons with heart disease. A pet can stave off loneliness giving lots of consistent, uncomplicated love. If fear of rejection causes you to retreat, now is the time to give up your need for approval—it's nice to have, but you can live without it. Fill your surroundings with music, flowers and good things to read.

Engagement turns loneliness into solitude. Your heart does not mind being alone, but it doesn't do well when it's lonely.

71

"Over the last two weeks how much have you been bothered by feeling stressed in life? Not at all, a little, moderately, or severely?" This is one of five questions from a new screening tool (Stop-D, Young, et al., 2007) designed to identify psychosocial distress in heart patients. The scale's author reports that emotional factors equal smoking as a health risk and have almost twice the negative impact on the cardiovascular system as high blood pressure.

According to the American Psychological Association almost half of all Americans believe their stress levels have increased over the past five years. Concerns about money and work lead the list of stress-producing triggers. Apprehension is rising along with rent and mortgage costs.

During the past 25 years the miracles of science and medicine have given us a chance to meet heart disease head-on, extending and saving lives. But now, to deal with all this additional stress, we eat poorly, stare for hours at a television or computer screen, or drink more than we should. Are we turning the clock back?

Stress is no big deal. Everybody I know is stressed. You can't do anything about it anyway. Yes, you can. And it is a big deal. Ask someone who has had a heart attack as a result of living with chronic stress.

Common stress triggers:

Commuting to work. What you can do:
1) Listen to audio books as you drive.
2) When traffic is delayed, take slow, deep breaths.
3) Think of how grateful you are to have a job.

Never getting caught up. What you can do:

1) Accept the idea that no one gets caught up.
2) At day's end, think of what you've done, not what's left to be done.
3) Ask "how important will this be next year?"

72

It's become second nature to begin calls, notes and emails with "I just had a minute … " or "I know how busy you are, but … " reflecting a new awareness or watchful vigilance to the many demands of life and resulting scarcity of time.

The efficiency of technology means we're able to find unlimited amounts of material on the Internet, saving ourselves a trip to the library. With a keyboard and a few clicks we ferret out more information in one minute than we might in one hour pulling documents and books off library shelves. Where did that time go—the time saved not going to the library? We order clothing, toys, books, music, movies, even groceries online. We don't have to run all over town to find these items. Where did that time go—the time saved skipping a trip to the mall? When you told yourself you would watch less television and create more quiet time. Where did that time go—the time saved as you reduced your hours glued to the tube?

You have a choice. When you save a minute or an hour you can fill that time with all the other tasks waiting in the wings—those things you've been meaning to get to—or you can use it for heart rest. So much is said about stress-management, but, as with regular exercise, how many of us take a sufficient amount of time to rest a hard-working heart?

In her book *The Heart Speaks*, cardiologist Dr. Mimi Guarneri gives mention to a study conducted over a 20-year period at the University of London that found "unmanaged reactions to stress were a more dangerous risk factor for heart disease and cancer than either smoking or high cholesterol." There's little disagreement: exercise, meditation, walking and yoga are tried-and-true stress buffers. However, there may also be great value in doing less.

Find the first day in your calendar when you have nothing scheduled. Across the page, in large letters, write *Not available today*.

Decide what peaceful, quieting activity you would like to do on that day—no work, no catching up, turn off your phone. Read, listen to calming music, work in the garden without a watch, doodle on a sketch pad, sit in a warm tub, make good use of the comfortable chair by the window as you think of all the people you love and all that's going well in your life.

73

As with many things in life, being prepared is good— in moderation. Buy gas before your gauge is on "E." Pick up groceries the day before the cupboard is empty. Insulate your house and get a pair of warm boots before winter blows in.

Planning ahead helps reduce the number of crises in your life and certainly lowers stress. But there's another type of planning that not only adds to stress levels, but can increase the likelihood of developing problems with your cardiovascular system: planning to be taken advantage of.

If you go through life expecting others' intentions toward you to be bad, the vigilant stance that goes along with the feared expectation can actually lead to inflammation, an immune response that can contribute to the build-up of plaque.

This is the avoid-harm-from-others/harm-myself paradox. You're so busy protecting yourself, making sure nobody takes advantage of you that your level of arousal will be elevated, wearing down your system.

Moderation is in order. Try to avoid jumping to conclusions about others. Try to maintain a reasonable perspective. Begin today looking for good to come your way.

74

Immediately following a health scare there's an acute awareness of one's behavior and anything about it that needs to change. Fear has a way of moving us to act and action offers a measure of control—control over whatever it is we fear most. *If I just do this or just do that, I'll be fine.* Fear gives way to determination.

A stressed, soft-around-the-middle couch potato can be transformed into a dedicated good-health devotee. In spite of a diagnosis of heart disease there can be joy and renewal. Suddenly your weight is down, exercise has increased, food choices have improved and you're managing stress better than ever. You hear yourself repeatedly uttering the words, *Let it go.*

Fast-forward six months after a heart attack or coronary artery bypass surgery—old habits reappear. Mindfulness slips into mindlessness. You forget to take your medication. Besides, you've been feeling so good lately. You haven't exercised for a few months because you've been too busy. No worries, you'll get back to it as soon as you get caught up. You're eating sugary desserts more frequently. After all, you've been so good for so long.

Do you recall what went through your mind at the moment you were given the diagnosis of heart disease? What were your plans? What goals did you set to reclaim your health, secure your independence and save your life?

They're still good goals. Time has a way of dimming fear and easing the disbelief you felt when you heard your doctor say, "You had a heart attack." If fear was once the motivation for change, what will motivate you now? Your children? Spouse? Unfinished work? The wonder of life? There must be something …

75

You scrutinize people, searching for something you can disapprove of: *She's overweight. He talks too much. She shouldn't wear white. Why does he pronounce that word that way? She just doesn't understand.*

Criticism creates distance. *You and I are different. We can't connect. I don't like what you said, the way you dress, the way you think, your political leanings, your religion or your table manners.* Existing relationships erode and new ones are hard to make. The heart suffers in isolation.

The next time you hear yourself finding fault with someone, search for something to admire or respect. You may be surprised at how quickly negative thoughts and feelings dissolve when you search for good.

Time is limited. What's the best way to use it?

76

At the end of a discussion with a cardiac-support group that included lots of contradicting points raised about food, exercise, stress and heart disease, I finished by saying, "Just use your common sense." A woman in the back of the room raised her hand and asked, "What if you don't have common sense?" The look on her face revealed the sincerity in her question.

I realized how naive I had been thinking everyone has an inner compass to guide them when things get confusing. And there are constantly new health studies emerging with views diametrically opposed to those presented just a month earlier. Who can you believe? What's the right answer?

A recovering heart patient will get as much medical and health supporting information as he or she can find. But it's important to listen to more than one idea before making decisions, to work openly and cooperatively with caregivers, and to ask questions.

Also, health is about the basics:

Moderation: not too much or too little of anything.

Balance: avoid jumping on every bandwagon heralding the next great thing that will make you as good as new.

What you know (what your grandmother knew): fresh fish, fruits and vegetables.

Simplicity: rest, peace of mind, quiet.

Movement: gardening, walking, stretching, swimming.

It's not that you don't know enough. You may have been given more information than you need to stay healthy.

77

People with heart disease are living longer, but not necessarily better, and those reporting the poorest quality of life are between the ages of 18 and 49. No one expects to be diagnosed with heart disease when life is just getting started. Still, while improvements in prevention and treatment are saving lives, the number of young people showing up in doctors' offices with hypertension and elevated cholesterol is growing.

Heart disease has always been thought of as a problem for the older man who had let himself go, or the aging woman, frail and with a complicated medical history. But a 20-year-old student? A 35-year-old mother with small children? The physical and emotional limitations of heart disease may be harder to accept when such high levels of vitality are expected and needed in our early years.

One way to define quality of life is by how able a person is to enjoy normal life activities. Being young and being active are synonymous. To be active you need stamina and with heart disease, that might be limited.

If you're young and unable to do the activities you were recently enjoying, the loss can be deeply felt. It's difficult for the older person, but a certain amount of loss of vigor is experienced as we age. No so when we're young.

Find what it is you can do, not what you can't do.

78

One sign of physical fitness is how quickly an individual's cardiovascular response returns to baseline following intense demand. Resiliency, a type of emotional fitness, confers the same benefit of fast recovery, bringing blood pressure and heart rate back to normal under conditions of negative emotional stress.

There may be a few ways to develop your own resiliency:

One is to be aware of your thinking habits and make every effort to lean toward the positive. According to positive psychologist and researcher Dr. Barbara Frederickson, the better you feel, the better your ability to see the big picture, aided by "flexible, broader thinking (2005)." This is what it means to maintain perspective, an important aspect of resilience.

A second method: In the classroom Dr. Frederickson had students keep a month-long daily record of their "best, worst, and seemingly ordinary events of the day." Some of the students were asked to add their comments regarding the "positive meaning and long-term benefits" found in each recorded event. At month's end, the "benefits and meaning" group showed signs of increased resiliency.

I doubt that anyone would turn down the opportunity to be able to bounce back after every disappointment, every hurt, every failure. Resiliency is a skill that can be nurtured.

79

The original Cynics, ancient Greek philosophers, spent their days expressing contempt for things pleasurable or easy. The modern-day cynic has eagerly expanded the list of things worthy of alienation or mockery. Today there's more to criticize, more to reject, more reasons to be close-minded.

Nobody knows if the ancient Cynics suffered from cardiac disease; however, we do know that modern cynics do. If you're at risk of developing a heart problem or if you've already been diagnosed with one, you can't afford to close your mind. You can't afford be suspicious of your doctor and to reject her advice. You can't afford to believe the negative publicity about the dangers of cigarettes is meant just to destroy the tobacco industry. You can't afford to use the excuse of your 98-year-old uncle, who never exercised and spent 40 years in front of the TV, for not taking care of your body. An open mind is a healthy mind.

Each day for one week tell yourself the following: *There is much I don't know. Let me listen. Let me take in everything. Let me consider all sides of the story.*

80

When people smoke, they admit to knowing the dangers cigarettes pose to the lungs and heart. When people eat unhealthful foods excessively, they're aware of the risks associated with obesity. When people choose an hour of television over a walk in the park, they accept the perils of sedentary living. And then there are those who defend their right to be angry, knowing it probably does more harm than good.

In the 1960s, '70s and '80s therapists began talking with patients about the right to express their feelings. The idea back then was: *My feelings are my feelings. I should be able to have them if I want to.* Some of that mentality lingers today, when patients in cardiac-support groups argue for their right to be angry and anything less is "ridiculous," "unreal," "impossible" or "just plain dumb."

What does anger have to do with "rights?" How sensible is it to be easily, frequently or intensely angry? Sure, I have the right to walk across the street, but it doesn't make much sense to cross when the stoplight turns green and cars zoom past.

If a mugger tries to steal your wallet, your anger will trigger physiological changes that can serve you well if you try to fight back for your property. Heightened emotions allow you to feel stronger, bigger and less fearful. Anger, when used appropriately, can help you act against injustice.

There will be times that you feel anger. But anger isn't a "right." It's a tool to be used wisely and only when absolutely necessary.

81

It's remarkable that we're ever in a happy place when you consider the endless number of strings we attach just to get there: *I'll be happy … When I feel more secure. When I earn more money. When I get married. When I get divorced. When I get my degree. When I've paid off my debt. When I get a job. When I retire.*

In his book *Happiness Now* Robert Holden, Ph.D., says we put limits on happiness, but we've also "grown accustomed to hiding it." Indeed, it seems when you tell someone you're happy they may see you as someone out of touch with the serious nature of life, or think you're not being truthful or that you're in denial. Holden goes on to say that in spite of having the tools to increase the amount of happiness experienced in the present, people decide "to stay put," attached to the familiar.

Examples of happiness beliefs, expressed by heart patients are: *I'll be happy when I'm able to reduce the amount of medication I have to take. I'll be happy when I can travel again. I'll be happy as soon as I get back to work. When I get over this fatigue. When I don't have to depend on my family any more.*

Happiness is expected to arrive after some optimal goal has

been reached. Why wait? If happiness comes first, it could play a significant role in helping you accomplish what you wish for faster and in a better frame of mind—starting immediately. We take better care of ourselves when we're happy. The result? Faster recovery, allowing you to feel more energetic, go back to work, regain your independence and take that vacation you've been dreaming about. That's the way it works. As Dr. Holden writes, happiness *now*—not *when*.

82

These days we hear of outstanding organizations providing workplace perks such as babysitters, dry-cleaning pick-up and delivery service, midday massages or a fully equipped gym. Everybody wins. Employees are healthier, health costs and absenteeism are down, productivity and morale are up.

Unfortunately, too many jobs require that you sit at your desk most of the day with too few breaks. Sitting at a desk, hour after hour, year after year, especially if your job is stressful, can be the start of many physical and emotional problems.

Here's something you might try and it's better for your heart than a pair of pressed pants: practicing yoga and meditation during lunchtime. Researchers have been studying how this helps employees. The idea isn't new, but measuring the benefits in the workplace is. Perhaps you and your coworkers can hire a certified yoga instructor who will lead you through 20 or so minutes of yoga and meditation.

One of the keys to good health is each day doing something small but positive for your body. After all, that's the way excess weight, stiff joints, clogged arteries and high blood pressure occur, dangerously accumulating little by little each day.

83

Your opinions are not always correct, but your mind processes them as if they were. If, after having a heart attack, you see your illness as chronic, difficult to manage and having a negative impact on your life, you may experience more fatigue than those who see their illness in a positive light and take a purposeful role in recovery.

Of course, the first thing to do is discuss tired feelings with your physician. If he or she tells you that medical recovery is proceeding as it should, the next step would be to consider your outlook. Is this the beginning of the end—or the beginning?

Approximately 80% of the development and progression of heart disease is related to lifestyle. That is, what you eat, whether or not you smoke, are sedentary and how well you manage stress and anger. Failing to consider the enormous impact behavior and emotions have on heart health; external factors such as prescribed medications and genetic history are often relied upon more than personal input when it comes to recovery.

With a take-charge approach to your illness, you're less likely to experience it as a never-ending problem that will forever reduce the quality of your life. Medicine matters, your father's heart disease matters and, perhaps, fate matters as well. But what you do makes a difference. If the statement, "I'm tired" has become a habit, replace it with "I'm … energized … improving … enthusiastic … feeling great … alive."

84

There's no shortage of information available about the risks of isolation, especially for someone with heart disease, and especially during the first year after a cardiac event. There's also no shortage of information about the benefits of companionship, friendship, sharing, cooperation and support. Being alone is detrimental to your health and well-being. Support and companionship are protective, buffering the blows of stress and strife found in every life. If you're living alone it's a good idea to increase the amount of personal contact you have with others.

But it's not quite so black or white. Living alone is not the problem—it's how you do it and what it means to you. This helpful news comes from a study concluding that feeling socially disconnected is the culprit and it may have little to do with how many people are in your life.

We've all heard the saying "Lonely in a crowd." That crowd can be your family, coworkers or the community social club you attend. So if you're lonely despite having others around, it might be helpful to reevaluate the way you view everyone or rethink the way they view you. Would you be better off by yourself? The goal is to feel connected whether alone or with others.

If you are truly alone and long for companionship, let your loneliness be the feeling that motivates you to find others who long for friendship as much as you do. And for those who may have learned to question your choice about being alone and feeling just fine—it's OK. You can stop wondering if there's something wrong with you because you spend most of your time doing the things you love to do, feeling content to see others just once in a while.

Remember: It's not about being alone or with others, it's about how you feel with the life you're living, the life you've created for yourself. Take care of yourself each and every day. The more pleased you are with your life, the easier it is to do just that.

85

I can't say "no." It's too risky. If I don't do what people want me to do, they won't like me. If I don't do it their way, they'll be mad. A nice person always helps. If someone asks me to do something and I refuse, I feel miserable!

When these are the rules you live by, resentment and guilt become familiar companions. If you were to stray from these principles, people won't need you. If people don't need you, why would they want to be with you? The cycle continues: You say "yes" when you long to say "no." You receive positive feedback and for an hour or a day you're safe—people still like you. You won't be abandoned.

Are all those "yeses" working for you? No, they're working against you.

So what's the connection to heart disease? When you can't say "no," you leave zero time to care for yourself. When you constantly do things you don't want to do, you experience what's known as a "slow burn." It's a type of anger that might not be obvious to the people you're with, but it's a physiological reaction that's happening within your body—vascular constriction and muscular tension make you feel exhausted.

Try this: For the next month respond to requests for help with, "May I think about it?" or "May I get back to you?" This response will help you cope with the discomfort you feel when you're put on the spot. It's anxiety born out of conflict between what you've been taught—help others—what your ancestral biology suggests—cooperate and we all survive—and what you would like to do—have time for yourself.

On the drive home, or as you walk your dog, consider what it is you've been asked to do. Ask yourself, *Do I really want to do this?* If you respond in the affirmative, the next questions should be, *What is my motive? Am I doing this because I really want to, or because I want this person's approval? What will it mean to say "no?" What's the worst thing that can happen if I say "no?"*

Perhaps now is a good time to practice saying "I'm sorry. I would love to, but I can't."

86

After a former patient's sudden, untimely death from a heart attack, I asked myself what could have contributed to such a tragedy. A quote by America's first professor of psychology, William James, came to mind: "The art of being wise is the art of knowing what to overlook."

The patient and I had met for less than six months. He was convinced that his life would be more satisfying if others would change: If only others would be more grateful (for him), more appreciative (of him) and pay more attention (to him). He spoke of the length of time a colleague had kept him waiting. He recalled how wrong it was for a friend to disagree with him. He described his frustration when, in evenings, his fiancé took time away from him to speak with friends on the phone. He grew angry if he thought he had been criticized. The more distance he kept from others, the more isolated he felt. Accepting flaws in others would mean facing his imperfections.

There isn't time to wait for everyone else to be what or how we think they should be. Acceptance begins now.

If this man could return for a day, I wonder what would matter most to him. Would he spend the day finding fault with canceled trains, late people or poorly prepared food? Or would he spend his precious moments gazing into his wife's face, finding kindness, love and beauty? Would he hold his infant daughter and see perfection?

She entered the world just 10 days after his death.

See what is good, beautiful and extraordinary. Now is your chance.

87

"Give sorrow words. The grief that does not speak whispers the o'er-fraught heart and bids it break."
William Shakespeare

Sorrow is felt by the man who lost some part of himself after a heart attack, or the woman who grieves for a partner who died from heart disease, and by the many caregivers who have developed a cardiac problem after years of caring for a dying friend or relative. The massive heart attack experienced by a parent grieving the loss of a child had its beginnings in sorrow.

What the medical community knows about preventing heart disease, then repairing the heart once its been damaged, is remarkable. Still, there is sorrow. There is sadness and an ache in the heart called grief.

With all we know, there is nothing to replace the experience of someone listening to what you need to say. Let them hear you.

88

Impatience is more than the leg shaking and finger tapping you might observe in the person sitting next to you at the doctor's office. What you can't see are the non-verbal cues that shout, *I can't wait one more minute!*

Are you someone who has more and more things to do each day with no additional hours in which to do them? In the cardiac world, this condition is referred to as "hurry sickness." Or perhaps you're someone who thinks waiting is something you shouldn't have to do—your time is too important, you're too important. This is known as "entitlement."

Waiting will test the impatient and close in on the anxious. The mind races ahead, thinking of all that must be accomplished in the next hour, the next week, the next year, making living in the "now" almost impossible. Personality has a lot to do with the how well people tolerate waiting, and a shortage of tolerance may contribute to the development of heart disease.

R. C. Roberts's definition of patience—the "ability to dwell gladly in the present moment, when one would rather be doing something else"—highlights what heart disease–prone people are missing: being glad. They're often irritable, fretful and sometimes even violent.

As a psychologist, I have met with cardiac patients whose impatience led them to dangerous extremes. One punched a stranger on a park bench, another jumped on the roof of a New York City taxi, another yanked a fast-food restaurant worker from the pick-up window. Each of these patients didn't get what wanted fast enough.

The more goal-oriented our society becomes, the greater our need to exercise our ability to wait. When our earliest ancestors ran from a tiger, they fully utilized the pumping adrenaline that gave them speed. Today, sitting in traffic with no possibility of movement releases the same adrenaline, but it has no place to go, wreaking havoc on your vascular system. We must all learn to "dwell gladly in the present moment."

89

A patient whose father had died years earlier came to see me. In the throes of severe cardiac arrest, this young man's heart had stopped beating. His cardiologist told him that he had "died on the table." During one of our meetings he said, "When I died, I saw my father. He told me it wasn't my time. I had to go back."

Whatever you believe about such experiences, they do happen, and often leave people feeling perplexed and unsettled. My 37-year-old patient asked what it was he was supposed to do with his life to make coming back worthwhile. At the time he was unmarried, living alone in a small apartment, working as a sales clerk in a liquor store. He began wondering if there was something more important for him to do than live a life that suddenly felt aimless and of little value.

Most of us, usually by our 50s or 60s, ponder questions of purpose. We ask, *Why am I here? What have I accomplished? Should I be doing more?* My patient, by circumstance, was forced to face these questions earlier in life.

According to C.R. Snyder and his colleagues (2005), we create meaning in life through our perception of the progress made while working toward our goals. The meaning of life and a person's "purpose" are personal and ever changing. A person raising a family may say that is her purpose. And she may also tell you that it changed dramatically when her kids left home. For someone else, purpose may be managing an organization that provides financial security for 500 employees and their families. For another, it may be volunteering at a homeless shelter.

Just what your goals are doesn't necessarily matter. What matters is that you have them.

90

Managing high blood pressure isn't easy. Sure, losing weight and exercising regularly can lead to a sizable reduction in readings, but if your pressure is too high, your doctor may still decide to prescribe pressure-lowering medication.

Here's something else to consider: There's an inverse relationship between blood pressure and positive emotions such as joy, enthusiasm and happiness. The more you have of one, the less you have of the other. And there's a positive relationship between negative emotions such as anger, depression, irritability and blood pressure. The more you have of one, the more you have of the other.

In 2006, Ostir, Berges, Markides and Ottenbacher conducted a study of more than 2,000 participants measuring the relationships between blood pressure and positive emotions. For the non-medicated group, raising positive feelings lowered both upper (systolic) and lower (diastolic) numbers. For those on medication, increasing positive feelings led to a decrease in diastolic pressure.

Some of us get lazy when a doctor gives us medication, assuming chemicals will do all the work. Just because you take a cholesterol-lowering drug like Lipitor or Zocor doesn't mean you can eat more cheeseburgers. For years the goal of therapy for depressed, anxious or angry patients was to help them reduce the frequency and intensity of their bad feelings. But it isn't enough to say, "I feel less sad than I did before." Now we know that good health, mental and physical, is protected in the presence of positive emotion.

Try this: Write a letter of gratitude and deliver it to someone in person. Perform an act of kindness for a stranger. Think of three things that went well today and ask yourself, *Why*?

91

Does having a corrective procedure for heart disease actually mean living a longer life? It may not. A patient's outcome is dependent on many factors: severity of disease; age; general health; how well a medical regimen is followed; obesity; and one's disposition.

Beginning in 1958 the National Institute on Aging followed about 2,400 people. Part of their investigation focused on the possible link between longevity and personality factors. It turns out that those who lived the longest scored the highest in measures of activity, emotional stability and conscientiousness. Those whose deaths were attributed to cardiovascular disease were significantly linked to the measure of emotional stability.

Today doctors record more instances of emotional instability in this country than at any time in history. We see more depression, anxiety, violence and stress.

After their procedures, the following people were technically cleared of risk: The person who lived alone, who, after having a heart attack, feared he would always be alone. He was soon found dead in his apartment. The person who was told that everything had gone well in her procedure, though she was still convinced that she would die of a heart attack. She did—on the street as she left the hospital. The person desperate to return to work, fearing that taking a few weeks off to recuperate would cause him to lose his clients. The person who had his computer and printer delivered to his hospital bed so no one would know he had had a massive heart attack. He wouldn't dare let his colleagues think he was away from his responsibilities, even for a minute.

Emotional turmoil is harmful to your health. How you find peace—therapy, exercise, getting together with friends, spirituality, daily naps—doesn't matter. What matters is that you find it.

92

Women live an average of seven years longer than men. A recent study found that most women are not able to enjoy these additional years of life without feeling lonely. Separateness turns into loneliness, adding to the list of factors that put women at risk for developing heart disease. In an article published in *Psychosomatic Medicine* (Thurston & Kubzansky, 2009), loneliness is described as, "The perceived discrepancy between actual and desired social relationships." Or the number of people a woman perceives as a part of her life, versus the number she might wish to have.

Solving this problem—finding more people to be with—isn't as easy as it seems. So much depends on where a person lives, how mobile she is, the state of her health, and how she's chosen to live her life up to now. But here are some ideas:

- Adopt a pet. If a dog or cat seems like too much trouble, get a fish or a small bird.
- Contribute to a foundation that helps support children in need. There are opportunities for this type of giving all over the world. Some organizations encourage a relationship with a particular child who will write to you, telling you of his or her progress.
- Send a weekly note of thanks to someone, anyone you can think of who has made a difference in your life.
- Plant a flower. If not in a garden, then in your windowsill.
- Buy a computer and learn how to e-mail. A computer allows instant connections with family members or former schoolmates, living thousands of miles away.

If someone were to offer you an additional seven years of life, could you refuse such a gift, contaminate it with negativity and despair, take it for granted as you allow it to slip away? Or would you look around to find something that's good, something that's beautiful, something that you can improve?

93

Placing complete trust in every person you meet might not be a good idea. But, if like many who eventually develop heart problems, your level of trust is so low it borders on cynicism, the very thing you do to avoid harm, may do harm.

If you regularly doubt the intentions of others, and even good deeds are met with suspicion—*What does this person want from me?*—being with people will be stressful. A doubting person is guarded, on alert, always assuming others will only do what's best for them.

When this happens, stress hormones are released. Fear of harm will activate the fight or flight response, raising blood pressure and circulating cholesterol. The association between people and discomfort fosters more and more social avoidance and isolation. Maybe there are thoughtless, insensitive people out there, but there are also caring and compassionate people. Tell yourself you won't jump to conclusions. Look for the good in those you meet.

94

Lack of social support may increase the risk of developing heart disease. Close connections with others are beneficial and multiply as the size of one's circle of support increases. But not just any kind of social relationship will do—quality matters.

In an *Archives of Internal Medicine* (De Vogli, et al., 2007) article, individuals involved in contentious relationships were found to have a 34 percent increased risk of suffering a coronary event compared to those in more satisfying relationships. It seems the absence of a confidante offering emotional support may actually increase cardiac vulnerability. In fact, there's evidence indicating that negative interactions may influence inflammatory, immune and metabolic reactions. In addition, when people are in turmoil, worry can replace the planning and goal setting associated with consistent, positive health routines.

For the quality of your relationships and the health of your heart, try this:

- Avoid being critical. Think before you speak. At the start of each day rehearse the way you'll respond to anticipated conflict. Just because someone says something unpleasant doesn't mean you must react with more negativity.
- Improve your listening skills. When the person you care about makes an effort to talk to you, stop what you're doing,

make eye contact, nod to show your interest, avoid the need to dismiss or "top" what they've said, look for something to agree with and respond with words that signal understanding.

- At the end of each day tell the person you care about something positive you noticed them do or say. Watch their reaction.
- Let no day go by without a kind gesture.

95

"Anger blows out the lamp of the mind."
William James

People continue to question the link between anger and the development of heart disease, or anger and cardiac-related death. There are hundreds of studies supporting this relationship, but still others that suggest the connection is weak, if it exists at all. So what's the truth?

Use common sense as you sort out contradictory information. After reading an article that argues there's no relationship between anger and heart disease, perhaps you'll allow yourself to be as angry as you like, whenever you like. But you know how physically depleted you feel following a bout of intense fury. Expressions such as "my blood boiled," "blind rage" or something "leaving a bitter taste in my mouth," speak volumes about what anger does to the body. You don't need scientific evidence to prove the toll anger takes. Clenched fists, tight jaw, pumping heart, bellyache and obsessive thoughts—these reactions say plenty.

If you believe you'll be dismissed or given a hard time when you call the doctor's office about the error on your bill, the slow, steady boil of anger will begin as you think about the call, before you've even dialed a number. This is the time to say: *This phone call could go badly or it could go well. I can't predict the office manager's reaction.*

Whatever happens I plan to remain calm, competent and in charge of myself. This problem will be resolved. Getting angry isn't helpful and it's too hard on my heart. I'm not going to make this situation more important than it is.

Avoid over-generalizing or jumping to conclusions. Don't decide that the driver in the car next to yours is out to get you. There's no evidence to back that up. Besides, you don't know what's going on in that person's life.

With a small change in expectations and open-mindedness, you can create a more agreeable, less threatening world. Now, with your changed expectations, make that phone call and notice how your body feels.

96

Hardiness, according to Salvatore Maddi, is composed of three Cs: commitment, control and challenge. So hardiness isn't necessarily about being burly or tough, it's about your outlook. A committed person "remains involved—no matter how stressful things become." Someone who has control can "influence outcomes of events, no matter how difficult this becomes." An individual who is up for a challenge accepts stress as "a normal part of living."

Whether or not heart patients embrace the three Cs will, according to Maddi, pit them either on the side of "collapsing" or "thriving."

- To change a lifetime of unhealthy habits, such as giving up unhealthful foods or sticking to an exercise regiment, commitment is necessary. Are you ready to make a commitment? Does "remaining involved" mean pledging to yourself and those who love you to whole-heartedly change your ways no matter what?
- You exercise control as you perceive your cardiac event as an opportunity to care for your health as never before. Influencing

your health may mean asking your doctor questions, even if it makes you uncomfortable to do so. It might mean learning all there is to know about how your heart functions. No control means higher blood pressure, lower levels of good cholesterol, a larger waistline, more triglycerides, less energy and continuing decline.

- Accepting stress as a normal part of life allows you to stop asking why, but instead facing the challenge with a take-charge attitude. You can't feel sorry for yourself. Heart disease isn't about fairness—it's almost entirely about the way you live.

97

World-class athletes use visualization to improve their performances. Imagination is an extraordinary tool with almost unlimited potential. According to Dr. Norman Doidge, the brain is "malleable, and perfectible by well-directed mental exercise." Imagining and putting into words your vision of a satisfying future may have a profound affect on your performance of everyday life

In 2006 Drs. Kennon Sheldon and Sonja Lyubomirsky asked study participants to write about their "best possible selves" for four weeks. This exercise had previously been found to increase positive mood and subjective well-being, and decrease illness. In the recent study subjects were instructed to outline what they would have done to reach their goals and to "identify the best possible way that things might turn out."

Improving mood can be accomplished by being appreciative and kind, and engaging in rewarding activities. Feeling positive about the future isn't necessarily difficult to achieve—at least for the short-term. But achieving long-lasting happiness and contentment, according to Sheldon and Lyubomirsky, may require "persistent effort" and the use of exercises that "fit" well with your personality.

The best possible selves study exercise was self-sustaining, feeding motivation while also improving mood. This is valuable information for heart patients whose dedication to optimal self-care may falter around six to eight months after a cardiac event.

Those 79 million people in the United States diagnosed with cardiovascular disease may struggle with the motivation and commitment necessary to stay healthy. That's where the best possible selves exercise, if carried out daily for at least four weeks, can help, improving moods and changing people's lives.

How to achieve your best possible self?

- Writing about renewed vitality and interest in life. Perhaps you can see your body grow stronger as you exercise several days each week.
- Imagining yourself riding a bicycle, playing golf or swimming each day.
- Describing the enjoyment of heart-healthy meals as you see yourself experimenting with a variety of fruits and vegetables.
- Noting how you'll respond to others with confidence rather than anger or aggression. Or how successfully you'll manage stress as you become more patient and tolerant.
- Seeing yourself with a new hobby, better friendships, closer family ties—anything that leads to a more satisfying, rewarding life.

Just imagine.

98

When you're satisfied, content, pleased and feel good about life your cardiovascular system gets a rest—vessels relax, blood flows easily and blood pressure decreases.

Behavioral scientists Ken Sheldon and Sonja Lyubomirsky found that people's well-being improved when they engaged in kind acts. Those who show greater interest in helping others and behave courteously, rate themselves as generally "happy."

In one of Sheldon and Lyubomirsky's studies, participants were asked to carry out five random acts of kindness weekly for six weeks. They wrote thank-you notes, visited ailing relatives and friends, donated blood and offered various types of help to others. The study subjects' levels of happiness and overall well-being increased. What good deed will you do today?

99

I recently met a woman committed to being assertive, who declared she could no longer be her three-year-old granddaughter's regular babysitter. I met a proud, determined man who announced that he hadn't smoked for three months. I met a woman who persisted in asking her doctor to administer a cardiac stress test, which saved her life, as he continued treating her for asthma. I met another woman who faced a potentially fatal brain tumor 15 years earlier, but is so appreciative of her gift of extra years, she remains resolute as she battles a new health challenge. I met a man whose ability to practice acceptance allows him, at 92, to embrace the idea that "things won't get much better" while relishing the "information filled" life he has lived so far.

And there were others—all with stories of how experiencing heart attacks, coronary bypass surgery, stents or valve replacements opened the door to positive change. They all had to make difficult lifestyle adjustments, but still found gratitude, growth, new-found freedom and personal strength.

These people developed heart disease because of smoking, sedentary living, stress, genetic makeup, obesity and complications associated with diabetes. But they're now protected because they can see past heart disease, lessening the risk of a future cardiac event.

According to scientists, one reason that may explain this lowered risk is the ability to see and feel something good in the midst of something bad, allowing for "a more adaptive daily cortisol pattern." Excess cortisol, also known among doctors as the "aging hormone," is associated with plaque development, inflammation, metabolic complications and damage to artery walls resulting from arousal and turbulent blood flow. Moskowitz and Epel (2006) found that, "Perhaps those for whom positive emotion is based on or drawn from the perceptions of an enriched life in the wake of a stressful event are those most likely to experience more advantageous physiological outcomes."

If you've been diagnosed with heart disease or are experiencing some other difficult time in your life, what have you discovered? Are you closer to the people you love? Do you value life more than ever? Have you found something to feel good about?

100

Having a close relationship means having a healthy heart. Married people are healthier than singles. Living alone isn't good for your heart. Isolation increases the risk of heart attack.

Not necessarily.

A close, but distressed, relationship could be detrimental to the heart. A growing body of literature informs us of the dangers of relationships in conflict that offer little in the way of emotional support. These relationships tend to cause hypertension and an elevated risk of having a cardiac event.

Living alone isn't harmful if your life is satisfying, includes good health habits, and is viewed positively. In fact, whether living alone or with another person, purpose, appreciation, engagement and wisdom protect the heart, buffering it from the harmful effects of disappointment and strain that accompany life.

Plenty of magazines and best-selling books advise readers on how to survive the dissolution of a relationship, reflecting the assumption that ending a relationship will be a negative experience. Is that always the case? Not according to Gary Lewandowski and Nicole Bizzoco (2007).

Relationships are thought to help us be better people, and to help us grow emotionally. However, a relationship without the elements needed for "self-expansion"—the development of knowledge, identities, and capabilities—may be "low" in quality. The end of a low quality relationship may not mean a "loss of self." Separation may allow a "rediscovery of the self," personal growth and more positive feelings.

A potentially painful event such as ending a relationship, particularly with all the frightening unknowns, could ultimately bring as many positive changes as anticipated negatives. The message isn't to encourage separation, but to highlight a healthier lifestyle. The key is to keep what matters in perspective, examining your life enough to know how best to take care of yourself and to grow and flourish emotionally and physically.

101

The more frequently you experience positive feelings, the less time your heart will be exposed to the damaging effects of stress hormones. How to feel more positive? Practice thinking from a position of abundance—focus on what you have, not on what's missing.

In a study investigating levels of happiness in two towns, the population found to be most content had the fewest choices of available goods. The townspeople with a greater variety of retail stores, from simple to luxurious, weren't as happy, and were less satisfied with their lives. These people compared themselves to others, and were exposed to material goods that they couldn't have or afford. But the happier townspeople believed that what they saw was well within their reach.

Bibliography

Albert, C. (2005) Phobic anxiety increases heart disease death risk among women. *Circulation: Journal of the American Heart Association;* 1111,480-487.

Biddle, S.J.H., Fox, K., Boutcher S.H., et al. (2000) The way forward for physical activity and the promotion of psychological well being. In S.J.H. Biddle, K. Fox & S.H. Boutcher (Eds.), *Physical Activity and Psychological Well-being* (pp.154-168). London: Routledge

Blumenthal, J.A., Babyak, M.A., & Moore, K.A. (1999) Effects of exercise training on older patients with major depression. *Archives of Internal Medicine;* 159; 2349-2356.

Clarke, J.S., Lindsay, D.R., & Sternberg, R.J. (2007) Implicit theories of courage.
The Journal of Positive Psychology, 2(2):80-98.

Davidson, K. & Prkachin, K. (1997). Optimism and unrealistic optimism have an interacting impact on health-promoting behavior and knowledge changes. *Personality and Social Psychology Bulletin,* 23, 617-625.

Denollet, J. (1998) Personality and coronary heart disease. The type-D scale -16 (DS-16). *Annals of Behavioral Medicine,* 20, 209-215.

DeVogli, R., Chandola, T. & Marmot, M.G. (2007) Negative aspects of close relationships and heart disease. *Archives of Internal Medicine;* 167:1951-1957.

Doidge, M.D., N. (2007)*The brain that changes itself: Stories of personal triumph from the frontiers of brain science.* Viking, New York.

Doshi, J.A., Cen, L., & Polsky, D. (2008)Depression and retirement in late middle-aged U.S. workers. *Health Services Research,* 43:2; 693-713.

Eaker, E.D., Sullivan, L.M., Kelly-Hayes, M., et al. (2007) Marital status, marital strain, and risk of coronary heart disease or total mortality: The Framingham offspring study. *Psychosomatic Medicine,* 69, 509-513.

Emmons, R.A. (2003) Personal goals, life meaning and virtue: wellsprings of a positive life., In C.L. Keyes & J. Haidt (Eds.). *Flourishing: Positive psychology and the life well lived.* (pp.105-128). American Psychological Association; Washington, D.C.

Frederickson, B.L. (2005) The broaden-and-build theory of positive emotions. in F.A. Huppert, N. Baylis, & B. Keverne, (Eds.) *The science of well-being.* (pp. 216-238). Oxford University Press, New York.

Guarneri, M. (2007) *The heart speaks.* Touchstone: New York.

Harvard Health Publications.(2007) The healthy heart: Preventing, detecting, and treating coronary artery disease. Harvard Medical School.

Helgeson, V.S. & Fritz, H.L. (1999) Cognitive adaptation as a predictor of new coronary events following percutaneous transluminal coronary angioplasty. *Psychosomatic Medicine,* 61, 488-495.

Holden, R. (2007) *Happiness now: Timeless wisdom for feeling good fast.* Hay House, Inc.

Holman, E.A., Silver, R.C., Poulin, M., et al. (2008)Extreme stress reactions to 9/11 increase cardiovascular ailments by 50%. *Archives of General Psychiatry, 65 (1):11.*

Kubzansky, L.D., Sparrow, D., Jackson, B., et al. (2006). Angry breathing: A prospective study of hostility and lung function in the normative aging study. *Thorax, 61, 863-868.*

Langer, E. (2005) Well-being. Mindfulness versus positive evaluation. In C.R. Snyder, & S.J. Lopez (Eds.). *Handbook of Positive Psychology,* (pp. 214-230). Oxford University Press: New York.

Leahy, R. L. (2005) *The worry cure: Seven steps to stop worry from stopping you.* Harmony Books, New York.

Levine, M. (2007) Pollyanna and the glad game: A potential contribution to positive psychology.*The Journal of Positive Psychology* , 2(4), 219-227.

Lewandowski, G.W. & Bizzoco, N.M. (2007) Addition through subtraction: Growth following the dissolution of a low quality relationship. *The Journal of Positiove Psychology*; 2(1):40-54.

Lupien, S.J. & Wan, N. (2005) Successful ageing: from cell to self. in *The science of well being.* F.A. Huppert, N. Baylis, B. Keverne (Eds.) Oxford University Press, Inc., New York.

McMaster University (Dec., 2008) Medical terms worry more people than lay terms study finds. *Science Daily.* www.sciencedaily.com.

Maddi, S. (2004) Hardiness: An operationalization of existential courage. *Journal of Humanistic Psychology.* 44:279-298.

Marshall, J.M. *Keep going: The art of perseverance.* Sterling Publishing Co., Inc., New York.

Moskowitz, J.T. & Epel, E.S. (2006) Benefit finding and diurnal cortisol slope in maternal caregivers; A moderating role for positive emotions. *The Journal of Positive Psychology.* 1(2): 83-91.

Nakamura, J. & Csikszentmihalyi, J. (2002) The concept of flow. *The Handbook of Positive Psychology.* Snyder, C.R. & Lopez, S.J. (Eds.) pp. 89-105. Oxford University Press.

Ostir, G.V., Berges, I.M., Markides, K.S., & Ottenbacher, K.J. (2006) Hypertension in older adults and the role of positive emotions. *Psychosomatic Medicine, 68:* 727-733.

Park, N., Peterson, C. & Seligman, M.E.P. (2006). Character strengths in fifty-four nations and the fifty US states. *Journal of Positive Psychology,* 1(3): 118-129.

Peterson, C., Park, N. & Seligman, M.E.P. (2006). Greater strengths of character and recovery from illness. *Journal of Positive Psychology,* 1(1): 17-26.

Rate, C.R., Clarke, J.S., Lindsay, D.R. and Sternberg R.J. (2007) Implicit theories of courage. *The Journal of Positive Psychology,* 2(2): 80-98.

Roberts, R.C. (1984) The strengths of a Christian. Philadelphia: Westminster Press. In C.L. Keyes & J. Haidt (Eds.) (2003) *Flourishing: positive psychology and the life well lived.* American Psychological Association, Washington, D.C.

Roizen, M.F. & Oz, M.C. (2007) *You staying young. Free Press, New York.*

Sheldon, K.M. & Lyubomirsky, S. (2004) Achieving sustainable new happiness: Prospects, practices, and prescriptions. In P.A. Linley & S. Joseph (Eds.). *Positive Psychology in Practice.* pp. 127-145

Sheldon, K.M. & Lyubomirsky, S. (2006) Increasing positive emotions. *The Journal of Positive Psychology;* 1(2):73-82.

Shibeshi, W.A., Young-Xu, Y, & Blatt, C.M. (2007) Anxiety worsens prognosis in patients with coronary artery disease. *Journal of the American College of Cardiology, 49, 2021-2027.*

Snyder, C.R. & Sigmon, D.R. (2005) Hope theory. *Handbook of Positive Psychology.* (Eds.) Snyder, C.R., & Lopez, S.J. Oxford University Press.

Thurston, R.C. & Kubzansky, L.D. (2009) Women, loneliness, and incident oronary heart disease. *Journal of Psychosomatic Medicine.* 71(8):836-842.

Walters, K. (2008) Panic disorder and risk of new onset coronary heart disease, acute myocardial infarction, and cardiac mortality: cohort study using the general practice research database. *European Heart Journal, 29(24); 2981-2988.*

Weinstein, N.D. (1989) Optimistic biases about personal risks. *Science.* 246, 1232-1233.

Young, Q-R., Ignaszewski, A., Fofonoff, D & Kaan, A. (2007) Brief screen to identify 5 of the most common forms of psychosocial distress in cardiac patients. *Journal of Cardiovascular Nursing, 22,* 525-534.

BOOKS

O is a symbol of the world, of oneness and unity. In different cultures it also means the "eye," symbolizing knowledge and insight. We aim to publish books that are accessible, constructive and that challenge accepted opinion, both that of academia and the "moral majority."

Our books are available in all good English language bookstores worldwide. If you don't see the book on the shelves ask the bookstore to order it for you, quoting the ISBN number and title. Alternatively you can order online (all major online retail sites carry our titles) or contact the distributor in the relevant country, listed on the copyright page.

See our website www.o-books.net for a full list of over 500 titles, growing by 100 a year.

And tune in to myspiritradio.com for our book review radio show, hosted by June-Elleni Laine, where you can listen to the authors discussing their books.

mySpiritRadio